The Priestly Service

How We Walk in the Spirit

By:
Jeff E. Brannon

The Priestly Service
How We Walk in the Spirit

By Jeff E. Brannon

Printed in the USA.
ISBN-13: 978-1-969004-00-1
ISBN-10: 978-1-969004-00-1

Proof Productions

Moundsville, WV 26041

Cover art by Jeff E. Brannon.

Acknowledgments

Without my darling wife, Miranda, this book would never have taken form. Thank you for letting me bang away at my keyboard for hours on end and for always being my encouragement. The practical application section in each chapter was her idea, and it added so much depth. I love you deeply.

As for Jeffery Justice, you never stopped reminding me to get this Part Two of *The Priestly Garments* finished. Thank you, brother, for your persistence, humor, and support through it all.

Long before this book existed, my mom, Lynn Hobbs, started me writing on an old Underwood typewriter and taught me to put thoughts into words. You've always been my first editor and greatest encourager. Thank you, Mom. (Did I mention she has published 8 books?)

Keeping me sharp as a writer is my daughter, Jessica Todd, who reads critically, challenges me in love, and still cheers me on. Thank you, Jessica … and for those who haven't yet, check out her new book *Orchard: Sown Among Thorns!*

In every season of writing, our prayer partners and supporters at *The Way Remnant* have filled our lives with faith, laughter, and light. You make ministry joyful and remind me daily that we are walking this priestly path together.

Never once have I taken for granted your prayers and encouragement. You help carry this vision further than I ever could alone.

To each of you, thank you for walking in the Spirit with us and for keeping the fire of His presence alive in this generation.

His Word has proven true: He equips those He calls.

Every conversation, every prayer, and every moment of revelation has been part of His training for this priestly walk.

Special thanks to all of those who serve alongside me as guest who come on *The Way Remnant*. Together, we are building a place where truth and Spirit meet. Especially *Janice F. Baca* who contributed chapter 9 to this book. Check out her books on Amazon!

People who read, share, and live these teachings are more than readers … they are fellow priests, walking in His rhythm and carrying His presence.

If this book draws you nearer to Yehovah's fire, then every effort has been worth it.

Remember always that the true altar is your heart. Keep it tended. Keep it burning.

In Messiah, we have all we need to walk in purity, power, and purpose.

To Him be the glory forever.

(Did you find it?!?!)

Dedication

This book is dedicated to every believer who longs to know Yehovah more deeply, to those who hunger for His presence and desire to walk not by emotion or effort but by His Spirit.
 To the ones who rise early to pray, who linger when others rush away, and who seek to serve not for recognition but for love. You are the living altars where His fire still burns.

To the sons and daughters who refuse to settle for routine faith, who crave holiness, and who long to carry His presence into every moment of life, may you find here a reminder that the priesthood was never about ritual alone but about relationship.

This is your invitation and your commission: to serve as priests of the Living God, to guard the flame, to live with clean hands and pure hearts, and to walk daily in the rhythm of His Spirit.

May every page strengthen your devotion, deepen your surrender, and awaken your calling to minister before Yehovah in Spirit and in truth until His glory fills your life, your home, and your world.

Selah, Shema, & Shalom.

An Invitation to the Reader

Before you begin, I want to speak to you plainly.

This book is not only written to inform or challenge you. It is written because the Father is still calling people into covenant with Him. If you are reading this and sense a pull toward truth, toward repentance, or toward something deeper than religion, that matters.

From the beginning, Yehovah has desired relationship, not distance. Covenant has always been His way of restoring what was broken. When humanity turned away, He did not abandon us. He prepared a way back.

That way is Yeshua.

Through His obedience, His sacrifice, and His resurrection, reconciliation with the Father was made possible. Sin no longer has to define you. Separation does not have to be your future. Through Yeshua, forgiveness is real, restoration is offered, and new life can begin.

If you have never entered into covenant with the Father, you can begin now. Speak to Him honestly. Confess what you know is sin. Turn from it. Acknowledge Yeshua as the one sent by the Father to restore what was lost. Ask to be filled with His Spirit and taught His ways.

A Prayer to Begin Covenant

Father Yehovah,

I come to You honestly and without excuses.
I confess my sin and the ways I have walked apart from You.
I turn from those paths and ask for Your forgiveness.

I acknowledge Yeshua as the One You sent,
the Messiah through whom restoration and life are made possible.
Because of Him, I ask to be cleansed and brought back into
covenant with You.

Fill me with Your Spirit.
Teach me Your ways.
Give me a heart that desires truth, obedience, and faithfulness.
Strengthen me to walk the path You have set before me.

I place my life in Your hands and ask You to begin Your work in
me.
Let what is broken be restored, and let what is dead be made alive.

In Yeshua's name - Amen.

Welcome to the Kingdom of Yehovah. Through covenant in
Yeshua, you are no longer separated but brought near and called
to serve as part of a Kingdom of priests, set apart to walk in truth
and obedience. Walk forward with confidence, knowing the Father
is faithful to teach you His ways and complete the work He has
begun in you.

Table of Contents

Preface

When I wrote *The Priestly Garments*, I was walking through something Yah had been pressing on my heart for years. **The garments reveal who we are in Messiah**. They show identity. They remind us that when Yah looks at us through Yeshua, He sees us as clothed in holiness. But the garments are only half the picture. If the garments show us *who we are*, then **the priestly service shows us how to walk it out.**

I've always longed to see what this looks like in real life, not just as a theory, but as something fully lived out. Different camps seem to carry little pieces of the puzzle, but instead of sharing them, they guard their piece and build whole denominations around it. The problem runs even deeper: there's a fractured ideology of who Yeshua is. Some only see Him as Savior … the Lamb of God who takes away the sin of the world … and they fail to see Him as Lord or King. Still other groups only see Him as High Priest, as though He has only one duty. That's like an orchestra playing with only the trumpet section. While it may be beautiful in its own way, it does little to present the richness of the music when all the accompanying parts flow together. Yeshua is not "either/or" - He is all of these and more. Scripture paints a far fuller picture, and it reminds us that it is in Him we live, and move, and have our very being. That's not theology to memorize - it's a reality to walk in. This book takes a deeper (though not exhaustive) look at what priests do and how that connects to us walking in the Spirit today.

Now, let me give you a little backstory. *The Priestly Garments* came from a 45-minute sermon I heard thirty-six years ago. That message sparked a lifelong journey, and since then, I've been "the Garment Guy" - teaching, writing, and learning more as the Spirit reveals. This new book is the natural next step, birthed out of prayer, study, and an ever-growing fire in me to help others walk practically in Messiah. In recent years, more and more people have asked me for a guide - not just the identity part, but the "*how-to-live-it*" part. That's what this book aims to do: to open the Scriptures and trace out the patterns of service Yah gave, so we can walk after Messiah in a way that's both practical and Spirit-filled.

Now, before we get rolling, let me talk about balance. I want you to know up front: I'm not trying to load you down with rules, nor am I trying to launch you into some cloud of mystical vagueness. Both extremes miss the mark. Lean too far to one side and you end up dry and rigid; lean too far the other and you drift off into confusion. And yes - I like to joke that there are Fruit Loops on every cereal aisle. That usually happens when someone gets overly focused on one truth while ignoring the rest. Build your house on just one truth, and it will always be lopsided and bound to fall. My heart is to keep this book balanced, grounded, and genuinely useful for your walk.

So here's what I invite you into: a journey that takes the ancient priestly service and lays it alongside our calling as a royal priesthood in Messiah. You'll see how every detail - sacrifices, duties, patterns of worship - points to Him, and how it also teaches us to walk in His Spirit day by day.

I don't claim this book is exhaustive. It's not the final word on the priesthood. But it is a faithful exploration, rooted in Scripture, that I believe will encourage, instruct, and challenge you. My prayer is that as you read, you'll not just *learn* about the priesthood - you'll begin to walk more fully in it.

And with that, I leave you with the words of the priestly blessing out of Numbers 6:24-26

Yehovah bless you and keep you;
Yehovah make His face shine upon you and be gracious to you;
Yehovah lift up His countenance upon you and give you peace.

May His shalom - the wholeness that comes only from Him - cover you as you step into His service.

Chapter 1 Daily Offerings and Sacrifices

The rhythm of priestly life in ancient Israel began and ended with sacrifice. Before a priest ever taught, blessed, or entered into holy service, he first stood before the altar. Fire greeted him at dawn, and smoke carried the fragrance of devotion into the heavens at dusk. This wasn't an occasional event. It was the daily heartbeat of Israel's worship - a continual reminder that life with Yehovah requires constancy, not convenience.

The Morning and Evening Burnt Offering - A Life Bookended by Fire

Numbers 28:3-4 says:

"This is the offering made by fire which you shall offer to the Lord: two male lambs one year old without blemish, day by day, as a continual burnt offering. You shall offer one lamb in the morning, and the other lamb you shall offer in evening."

This daily burnt offering was called the *Tamid* (תָּמִיד, tamid, Strong's H8548) - meaning perpetual, ongoing, without interruption. A lamb in the morning. A lamb in the evening. Day after day, year after year, the altar never cooled, the flames never dimmed. Before a priest ate his first meal or tended to the needs of the people, he first laid a lamb upon the fire. And when the day closed, with its labors complete and its burdens heavy, he ended not with his own rest but with Yehovah's portion once more offered up.

The message is striking: a priest's life was bookended by surrender. His day was framed not by his own priorities but by Yehovah's presence.

And this, of course, points us straight to Yeshua. He is the Lamb offered "once for all" (Hebrews 10:10). His sacrifice was final, but its power is continual. Just as the altar fire never ceased, so His intercession for us never ends. Hebrews 7:25 declares that He "always lives to make intercession" for those who draw near. Morning and evening, Messiah Himself stands before the Father as our continual offering.

For us, the Tamid calls us into a daily rhythm of surrender. Every sunrise is an invitation to lay down our will, and every nightfall an opportunity to place the victories and failures of the day back into His keeping. Paul picks up the picture when he urges us to "present your bodies as a living sacrifice, holy and acceptable to God" (Romans 12:1). Unlike the lambs, we are not consumed in a moment. We are called to remain on the altar, continually surrendered.

Picture your own day like that of the priest. You rise, and before you grasp at tasks or appetites, you turn your heart heavenward: *"Here I am, Yehovah, Your portion before the sun rises."* And at day's end, you do not collapse under unfinished work or hidden failures. You lay them on the fire of His mercy: *"Here it is, Lord - my successes, my mistakes, my weariness. I offer it all to You."* To live like this is to live as a fire keeper - guarding the flame of devotion so it never grows dim.

The Incense Offering - Fragrance of Prayer

Exodus 30:7-8 says:

"Aaron must burn sweet incense on it. Every morning, when he trims the lamps, he must burn incense. When Aaron lights the lamps at sundown, he must burn incense on it. It is to be a perpetual incense before the Lord throughout your generations."

Morning and evening, just as the burnt offerings were laid on the altar, incense was burned on the golden altar inside the holy place. As fire consumed the spices, fragrant smoke rose upward and filled the sanctuary. This wasn't the smell of burning flesh but the sweetness of worship - a fragrance that set the holy place apart from the camp outside.

Scripture interprets incense as a picture of prayer. The psalmist cries, "Let my prayer be counted as incense before You" (Psalm 141:2). Revelation shows us golden bowls of incense in heaven, which are "the prayers of the saints" (Revelation 5:8).

But here's the thing: incense only gives off fragrance when it's crushed and touched by fire. The holy recipe in Exodus 30 required the spices to be ground fine, reduced to powder. Only when fire hit those crushed spices did their aroma rise to heaven. Prayer works the same way. Words alone aren't enough. Prayer becomes incense when it's pressed through humility and ignited by the Spirit's fire.

Yeshua embodied this. His life was saturated with prayer. He withdrew to lonely places, prayed with such intensity that His sweat became like drops of blood, and even now He intercedes for us without ceasing. He is the incense that never fades, the fragrance heaven never wearies of.

For us as priests in Messiah, the incense altar reminds us to "pray without ceasing" (1 Thessalonians 5:17). Not only set times of prayer in morning and night, but whispers of gratitude throughout the day, cries for mercy in the middle of struggle, songs of worship in the night, even groans too deep for words. A life pressed and set on fire becomes a fragrance Yehovah delights to breathe in.

The Grain, Oil, and Wine Offerings - A Pressed and Poured - Out Life

Every burnt offering was accompanied by grain mixed with oil and a drink offering of wine (Numbers 28:5-7). These were symbols of the fruit of human labor - bread and drink, the ordinary staples of life - offered back to Yehovah in worship.

The grain was never presented dry. It was mingled with oil, which in Scripture represents the Spirit's anointing. But oil only comes through pressing. Olives must be crushed to release it. At Gethsemane - "the olive press" - Yeshua sweated drops of blood as He surrendered to the Father's will. Out of His crushing came the outpouring of the Spirit for the world.

Wine was poured out beside the altar, never gathered back. Grapes, too, must be crushed before their richness flows. Yeshua took the cup and said, "This is My blood of the covenant, which is poured out for many" (Mark 14:24). His life was not given sparingly but poured out completely.

For us, this means embracing the pressings of life. Oil and wine still flow in the same way - through surrender. Paul put it plainly: "We are hard pressed on every side, but not crushed... we always carry in our body the death of Yeshua, so that the life of Yeshua may

7

also be revealed in us" (2 Corinthians 4:8-10). In our pressings, anointing is released. In our pourings, joy is multiplied.

Slaughtering Sacrifices - The Cost of Holiness

Leviticus 1-7 describes the details of slaughtering, draining, and burning sacrifices. It was bloody, heavy work. The priest was not a distant observer. He held the knife, smelled the blood, and saw life drain away. The altar was not a place of comfort - it was a place of death. And every sacrifice shouted the truth that sin has a cost.

All of this points us to Yeshua, the Lamb of God who takes away the sin of the world (John 1:29). He is both Priest and Sacrifice, both Offerer and Offering. The cross was not sanitized. It was blood, sweat, agony. Holiness costs something.

And it still does. Paul urges us to "put to death" the deeds of the flesh (Romans 8:13). Following Yeshua is not tidy or theoretical. It is hands-on. It means confronting sin, cutting away what does not belong, and agreeing with the Spirit that our lives belong to Him. Baptism reminds us of this - to be immersed into Messiah is to be buried with Him in death and raised with Him to new life (Romans 6:3 - 4). Once immersed, we cannot return to what we were before. We take on His nature, like a cucumber changed into a pickle in brine. His Spirit becomes the atmosphere we live in.

Offerings for Individuals - Meeting People at the Altar

The priests also received sacrifices from individuals - sin offerings, peace offerings, thank offerings. Each one represented someone's personal need, sorrow, or gratitude. The priest's role was to meet people at the altar and help them bring it before Yehovah.

Yeshua fulfills this perfectly. His sacrifice wasn't only for a nation but for each person. He knows His sheep by name. During His earthly ministry, He forgave sins, healed the broken, welcomed the outcast, and lifted burdens. He still meets us at the altar today.

And so do we, as priests in Him. Galatians 6:2 calls us to "bear one another's burdens, and so fulfill the law of Messiah." This means standing with brothers and sisters, carrying their sin, sorrow, and wounds to the altar of prayer. Sometimes it's interceding for forgiveness. Other times it's helping them lay down shame, grief, or trauma. To live as priests is to walk people into Yehovah's wholeness.

Messiah - Life Parallel: A Continual Offering

All of these daily duties converge in Messiah. He is our continual Lamb, our incense of intercession, our pressed oil, our poured - out wine, our High Priest, and our Shalom. In Him, we learn the rhythm of surrender, prayer, pressing, sacrifice, and intercession. In Him, we learn to live as daily offerings - "living sacrifices, holy and acceptable to God" (Romans 12:1).

Teaching Takeaways - Daily Offerings and Sacrifices

- The Tamid teaches us to begin and end every day with surrender.

- The incense altar calls us to cultivate a life of prayer.

- The grain, oil, and wine offerings remind us that anointing and joy flow through pressing and pouring out.

- The slaughtering of sacrifices shows us holiness is costly - sin must die.

- The offerings for individuals call us to bear others' burdens and walk them to the altar of Messiah.

Reflections for the Reader

- How might I bookend my day with surrender?

- Do my prayers rise steadily like incense, or only in crisis?

- Where am I being pressed or poured out, and how might Yehovah be releasing oil or joy through it?

- What "deeds of the flesh" do I need to lay on the altar?

- How can I better serve others by helping them bring their burdens to Messiah?

How to Walk This Out Practically

- Start and end your day with surrender.

- Build pauses for prayer throughout your day.

- Embrace the pressings of life as opportunities for anointing.

- Put sin to death daily, practicing confession and repentance.

- Be willing to live poured out, serving and giving joyfully.

- Carry others to the altar, standing with them in prayer until they find wholeness in Messiah.

Prayer Activation

"Yehovah my God, I step onto the altar today.
Let my mornings and evenings be marked by surrender, my life framed by Your presence.
Let my prayers rise like incense, pressed by humility and ignited by Your Spirit.
In my pressings, release oil. In my pourings, release wine.
Baptize me again into the death and resurrection of Yeshua, that I may carry His fragrance and His life.
Make me a priest who carries others to Your mercy, who helps lift burdens, who speaks forgiveness and healing.
Yehovah Shalom, bring wholeness to my broken places, and teach me to walk with others until they find completeness in You.
Here I am, pressed, poured out, surrendered.
In Yeshua's name, amen."

Chapter 2: Maintaining Temple and Priestly Cleanliness

The service of the priests in the Tabernacle and later in the Temple was not only about sacrifice and offering. It was equally about holiness. Every action, garment, and ritual pointed to a God who is pure and who calls His servants to guard that purity. Cleanliness was not optional. It was essential. To serve in the presence of Yehovah meant keeping both body and soul consecrated.

Keeping the Garments Clean and Holy

Moses was commanded, "And you shall make holy garments for Aaron your brother, for glory and for beauty" (Exodus 28:2). These garments were not ordinary clothing. They were set apart for sacred purpose. Every thread carried meaning. The linen tunic, breeches, sash, and turban symbolized purity and separation unto Yehovah. Even the materials reflected divine intent, for linen does not cause sweat, showing that the priest's service was to be done in rest, not in the strain of the flesh.

Yet priestly work was far from clean. They served in the desert where dust clung to everything. They handled the blood of sacrifices, trimmed the wicks of the lamps, and worked around the altar and the table of showbread. They helped lift, wash, and prepare offerings, assisted others in their worship, and often left the sanctuary carrying ashes or refuse from the holy place. In the course of faithful duty, their garments would inevitably become soiled. Getting dirty did not always mean sin; sometimes it simply meant service. Holiness did not isolate the priests from the realities of their work; it taught them how to stay pure in the midst of it.

Scripture gives careful attention to how the priests were to handle their garments. When a priest removed the ashes from the altar, he was to change his garments before carrying them outside the camp (Leviticus 6:10-11). This act made a clear distinction between service performed before Yehovah and ordinary duties beyond the sanctuary. Holiness was not a general attitude; it was a visible way of life.

The clean garments reminded both priest and people that holiness could be seen. A stained robe spoke of neglect, while spotless garments testified of care, diligence, and reverence. In the same way, our spiritual garments, our conduct, words, and attitudes, reveal the condition of our hearts before Yehovah. What we wear before Him is not fabric but character.

To keep these garments clean, we must continually wash in the Word. Paul writes that Messiah sanctifies His people "by the washing of water with the Word" (Ephesians 5:26). Just as water removes dirt from the body, the Word removes impurity from the soul. It cleanses our thoughts, renews our motives, and refreshes our hearts. When we read, study, and meditate on Scripture, the Spirit uses it to expose what does not belong and to restore what does. The priest washed his garments with water drawn from the laver; we wash ours with the living water of the Word.

Just as the priests were commanded to keep their garments clean, we are called to "put on the Lord Yeshua Messiah" (Romans 13:14) and to "walk in white" (Revelation 3:4). Every day presents the same choice: will we step into His presence clothed in purity, or will we approach with the stains of compromise? Holiness still matters. It is both inward and outward, both hidden and seen. A priest of Yehovah must be as careful with his spiritual garments as Aaron was with his linen ones, for we too are called to minister before the Holy One in glory and in beauty.

Bathing Before Service

Between the bronze altar and the Tent of Meeting stood the laver, a basin gleaming with water drawn for one purpose: cleansing. Exodus 30:18–21 commands that Aaron and his sons wash their hands and feet before they enter the tent or approach the altar, "that they may not die." This was no mere ritual. It was a command tied to life and death. The holy presence of Yehovah demanded purity, not pretense. Any stain, whether of blood or dust, was to be washed away before service began.

The laver served as a mirror of truth. As the priest leaned over its surface, he saw both his reflection and his need. Holiness was not assumed; it was maintained. Each washing reminded him that ministry before Yehovah required both outward and inward cleansing. What the hands touched and where the feet walked had to be sanctified before approaching the altar of the Living God.

This pattern pointed forward to the cleansing Yeshua gives His disciples. Before going to the cross, He washed their feet and said, "If I do not wash you, you have no part with Me" (John 13:8). He was not abolishing the laver's meaning but fulfilling it. The true washing comes not by water alone but by the Word and the Spirit. Paul echoes this when he writes that Messiah cleanses His people "by the washing of water with the Word" (Ephesians 5:26).

For us as priests in Him, bathing before service speaks of repentance and renewal. Before we minister, teach, serve, or intercede, we must pause to let the Spirit search our hearts and cleanse us from hidden impurity. Holiness is not automatic; it is intentional. Each time we come before Yehovah, we step first to the laver to confess, to be washed, and to remember that only the pure in heart will see God (Matthew 5:8).

Removing Ashes from the Altar Daily

Each morning, before anything else, the priest dressed in his linen garments and removed the ashes of the burnt offering (Leviticus 6:10-11). It was not a grand or public act. There were no crowds to see, no songs to mark the moment. Yet it was essential. The fire on the altar was never allowed to go out, but if the ashes from yesterday's sacrifice were left in place, they would smother the flame. Renewal required removal.

Those ashes represented what had already been given to Yehovah - yesterday's prayers, yesterday's repentance, yesterday's obedience. They were once holy, but if they remained too long, they became a barrier to what He wanted to do next. The same is true in our spiritual lives. Yesterday's devotion, no matter how sincere, cannot sustain today's fire. What was once vibrant can quickly turn into routine if we do not clear space for new surrender.

Paul understood this principle when he wrote, "Forgetting those things which are behind and reaching forward to those things which are ahead, I press toward the goal for the prize of the upward call of God in Messiah Yeshua" (Philippians 3:13-14). The things behind us can be failures or successes. Both can become ashes if we cling to them. Sin and shame weigh us down, but so can pride

15

in past victories or comfort in yesterday's revelation. The Spirit calls us to press on, to clear away both the guilt that condemns and the glory that distracts, so the altar of our heart remains open for fresh fire.

Every day brings a choice. We can live among the ashes of what was, or we can rise to tend the flame of what is being kindled anew. Removing ashes daily means refusing to live on old experiences, old moves of God, or old moments of repentance. It means starting each day with the humility to say, "Search me, Yehovah. Show me what needs to be cleared away."

When we do, the flame stays pure. The altar burns clean. The Spirit's fire finds room to breathe. Yesterday's offering made the altar holy, but today's surrender keeps it alive. Forgetting what is behind, we press forward, not backward into memory but upward into the continual presence of Yehovah.

The Fire from Heaven - Maintaining Yah's Fire, Not Strange Fire

When the Tabernacle was completed and the sacrifices were prepared, something extraordinary happened. Leviticus 9:24 records, "Fire came out from before Yehovah and consumed the burnt offering on the altar. When all the people saw it, they shouted and fell on their faces." The first flame that ever burned on the altar did not come from human hands. It fell from heaven.

That moment marked the beginning of priestly service. Every offering after that was to be consumed by the same holy fire. It was never to be replaced or replicated by another source. Yehovah's fire was sacred because it represented His presence, His approval, and His power. It was the visible sign that He had accepted both the altar and the priests who ministered there.

But just one chapter later, tragedy struck. Nadab and Abihu, the sons of Aaron, offered "strange fire" before Yehovah, and they died instantly (Leviticus 10:1-2). The text never says the fire looked different. It was strange because it was unauthorized. It did not come from the flame God had ignited. It was human fire brought into divine service.

True priesthood does not begin with human effort. It begins with divine fire. Ministry apart from the Spirit's flame may look sincere, but it is powerless. The priests were never told to create fire, only to keep it burning. In the same way, we are not called to invent zeal or stir up emotion, but to tend the fire that Yehovah has already kindled in our hearts.

Every generation faces the temptation to bring strange fire. In the medieval era, the Church introduced "moving statues" that wept or bled to stir emotion and draw crowds, often used to encourage indulgences rather than repentance. Centuries later, different forms of strange fire continued to appear—rituals and experiences meant to imitate the supernatural without the Spirit's power. In recent decades, feathers and gold dust have been claimed to fall in sanctuaries as signs of God's presence, yet often without true holiness or transformation following. Some have even gone so far as to create "Christian Tarot Cards" and "Christian Ouija Boards," rebranding divination as spiritual revelation. These are modern examples of the same deception Nadab and Abihu fell into, attempting to bring the fire of heaven by human means.

Strange fire is not always obvious. It can come through entertainment that replaces reverence, emotional hype that mimics the Spirit, or self-promotion dressed as ministry. Anything that seeks to substitute the presence of Yehovah with performance or counterfeit signs becomes strange before Him. The fire that pleases God still comes only from the altar He ignites, and it still burns in the hearts of those who serve Him with purity and truth.

The same is true for us. The moment you were filled with the Spirit, the fire of Yehovah fell upon your altar. It was not earned or manufactured; it was given by grace. Now your calling is to keep it burning. The fire must not go out. Prayer, obedience, and surrender are the wood that feeds it. Compromise, pride, and neglect smother it. The fire will only remain where reverence is maintained.

We must learn to serve from the fire, not for the fire. The difference is everything. When ministry flows from the flame of His presence, it carries life. When it comes from human zeal, it eventually burns out. The priests did not fan the flame to impress others; they guarded it so Yehovah's glory would remain among the people.

Every act of service must begin with His flame, not our own. Whether we teach, sing, lead, or pray, the question is the same: does the fire still come from Him? We are keepers of the flame, not creators of it.

Guard the fire. Do not let it fade. Do not replace it with something that shines brighter but burns colder. The same fire that fell in the wilderness still falls today, first upon the altar of the heart, and then upon every life surrendered to serve. Let it burn until the world knows the difference between strange fire and holy fire.

Purifying Themselves After Contact with Death or Uncleanness

Leviticus 21:1-8 commands the priests to avoid defilement by contact with the dead, except in the case of their closest family. Even in mourning, holiness was guarded. The priests were called to model separation from the corruption of death because they served before the God of life. Their lives were to reflect His nature, not the decay of the world around them.

This instruction went beyond physical death. It revealed a spiritual principle that runs through all of Scripture: death and life cannot dwell together. To stand before Yehovah meant to walk in the reality of His life-giving holiness. The altar was a place of fire and blood, yet never of corruption. Nothing dead could remain there.

Yeshua echoed this same call to separation when He said to a potential disciple, "Follow Me, and let the dead bury their own dead" (Matthew 8:22). He was not condemning compassion for family but exposing a deeper truth. Those bound to the ways of this world, its sin, its unbelief, and its spiritual deadness cannot walk in the life of the Kingdom until they leave death behind. To follow Yeshua requires a decisive break from the old order of things. Life cannot be mixed with death, holiness cannot be blended with compromise, and forward movement in the Spirit requires leaving behind what no longer lives.

We see this same principle when Yehovah appeared to Moses at the burning bush and said, "Remove your sandals from your feet, for the place where you stand is holy ground" (Exodus 3:5). Sandals were made from the tanned hides of dead animals. In that moment, God was teaching Moses a sacred truth: nothing touched by death could stand on ground made holy by His presence. The priest who approached the altar and the prophet who stood before the flame both had to remove every trace of death before they could draw near to the Living One.

I will never forget the first time I truly understood the smell of death. Growing up, I was always told to smell meat before cooking it to make sure it had not spoiled. I used to ask, "How will I know if it's bad?" and the answer was always the same: "Oh, you'll know." One day I found a package of beef cutlets that had been pushed to the back of the refrigerator. Thinking they would still be fine, I opened the package and instantly wished I hadn't. The stench that filled the air was overwhelming. My stomach turned, my eyes watered, and I nearly lost everything I had eaten for a week. The odor was unmistakable, thick with the sour rot of decay. Once you smell death, you never forget it.

That smell taught me something spiritual. Death always carries an odor, even when it hides behind the appearance of something once good. The same is true in our walk with Yehovah. Sin, bitterness, pride, or unbelief may look acceptable for a time, but left unattended, they begin to rot. The Holy Spirit recognizes it immediately, even when we do not. Just as my nostrils rebelled against the smell of spoiled meat, our spirit should recoil at the stench of sin and corruption.

Paul captures this calling when he writes, "We are to God the fragrance of Messiah among those who are being saved and among those who are perishing" (2 Corinthians 2:15). The lives of believers are meant to carry the scent of life itself, the aroma of holiness, purity, and devotion to Yehovah. Just as the incense of the sanctuary filled the Tabernacle with fragrance, our lives should fill the world with the sweet aroma of His presence. But that fragrance cannot cling to hearts still marked by death. Only when we cast off what is unclean and walk in His Spirit do we release the true scent of Messiah's life to those around us.

To walk in holiness is to choose life every day, to separate from what corrupts the soul and to draw near to the One who gives breath and renewal. When Yeshua said, "Follow Me," He was calling His disciples to the same purity the priests upheld, now empowered by His Spirit within. We no longer avoid death out of fear; we overcome it through His life. The God of life dwells in us, and through us He spreads the fragrance of Messiah into a dying world.

Messiah's Life Parallels: The True Fire of Heaven

All these priestly commands - washing, cleansing, removing ashes, guarding garments, and maintaining the altar fire - find their fulfillment in Yeshua, our eternal High Priest. He is not only the one who serves before Yehovah; He is also the altar, the offering, and the fire itself.

- **Clean garments** remind us of Yeshua's sinless life. Though He walked among sinners, He remained unstained, showing that holiness is possible even in a defiled world.

- **Bathing before service** reflects Yeshua washing His disciples' feet before the cross. He served from purity, not for it.

- **Removing ashes daily** parallels His constant communion with the Father. Yeshua often withdrew to pray, clearing away the distractions of the day so that His flame never dimmed.

- **The fire from heaven** points to Pentecost, when the same Spirit that empowered Yeshua fell upon His followers. The divine fire that once burned on the altar now burns within us.

- **Avoiding defilement by death** was fulfilled when Yeshua conquered death itself. The grave could not hold Him, and now those who follow Him walk in the power of life, not the shadow of decay.

In Messiah, we see perfect priestly service - pure, disciplined, and filled with heavenly fire. Every priestly act now flows through Him, and every believer who serves in His name carries that same fire into the world.

Teaching Takeaways

- The priests were not only cleansed but consecrated. Their purity prepared them to carry the divine fire.

- The fire that began from Yehovah could not be replaced by human zeal. True ministry flows from His presence, not emotion or performance.

- Strange fire still exists today when people attempt to imitate the Spirit's power without surrendering to His holiness.

- Holiness must be guarded in both action and intention. What begins as worship can become strange if disconnected from obedience.

- The believer's heart is now the altar. The same command applies: keep the fire burning, remove the ashes, and guard it with reverence.

Reflections for the Reader

- Has your spiritual fire been replaced by routine or emotion rather than true intimacy with Yehovah?

- In what ways might "strange fire" have tried to creep into your service, perhaps through pride, comparison, or performance?

- Are there practices, influences, or attitudes that look spiritual but lack the Spirit's power in your life?

- How can you rekindle the flame of pure devotion that once burned in your heart?

- What practical steps will you take to ensure the fire on your altar comes from heaven and not human effort?

How to Walk This Out Practically

- **Return to the source.** Seek the fire that comes from His presence, not from imitation or excitement. Ask Yehovah to reignite His flame in your heart.

- **Guard the flame.** Refuse to substitute entertainment or emotional hype for genuine encounter. Protect your time in prayer, fasting, and worship.

- **Test the spirits.** Measure every sign, teaching, or manifestation by the Word of God. If it does not lead to holiness, it is not from Him.

- **Serve from rest.** Linen garments do not cause sweat. Ministry should flow from the peace of being in right standing with God, not the strain of self-effort.

- **Walk in daily renewal.** Each morning, remove the ashes of yesterday - confess, release, and make room for new fire.

- **Carry His fragrance.** Let the aroma of your life testify that the fire still burns within you, bringing warmth, light, and purity wherever you go.

Prayer Activation

Father Yehovah, I thank You for the holy fire that fell from heaven and now burns within my heart through Your Spirit. Keep me from strange fire and false zeal. Let every act of my service begin with Your flame, not my own. Teach me to guard what You have kindled and to keep my altar clean and ready for Your presence. May the fragrance of Messiah flow from my life as a testimony of Your holiness and power. Let the world see Your light burning in me, pure and unending. In Yeshua's name, Amen.

Chapter 3: The Lampstand and the Light of Yehovah

Among the holy furnishings of the Tabernacle, the golden lampstand, or menorah, stood as a constant reminder of Yehovah's presence. Unlike the altar of burnt offering or the table of showbread, the lampstand was not associated with sacrifice or provision of food. Its function was light. Without the menorah's light, the priest could not see to move within the Tabernacle or to carry out his sacred duties. In the same way, without the light of the Spirit shining in us, we cannot see where to walk or perform our priestly service in Messiah.

To Israel, the menorah testified that Yehovah dwelt among them, and to the priests, it was a daily reminder of their responsibility to guard the flame of His presence.

The Menorah's Purpose and Design

Exodus 25 describes the intricate details of the menorah: pure gold, hammered work, with seven branches adorned with almond blossoms, buds, and flowers. This imagery pointed to life and fruitfulness, reminding Israel that Yehovah is the source of light and life. The menorah stood in the Holy Place, opposite the table of showbread, illuminating the bread of the Presence and casting light on the veil before the Most Holy Place.

The menorah's design was not accidental. The almond blossom was the first to bloom after winter, a sign of awakening and watchfulness. Jeremiah later saw a vision of an almond branch (Jeremiah 1:11-12) as a symbol of Yehovah's vigilance in performing His word. Thus the menorah proclaimed both the life of God and His faithful watchfulness over His people.

For us today, the menorah teaches that our lives must reflect His life and fruitfulness. Just as the almond blossoms reminded Israel that God was awake and watchful, we must remain spiritually alert, awake to His Word, and quick to respond in obedience.

Trimming the Wicks and Replenishing the Oil

Exodus 27:20-21 and Leviticus 24:1-4 commanded Aaron and his sons to ensure that pure olive oil was provided for the lamps, and that the wicks were trimmed daily so the light might never go out. The oil had to be clear, beaten from olives, free of sediment. Impure oil would cause the flame to sputter or smoke.

Each morning and evening, the priests entered the Holy Place to tend the lamps. They removed the charred portions of the wicks, replenished the oil, and made sure the light shone without interruption. This work was continual, day after day, year after year. The menorah was not ornamental. It was functional. Its light was to shine perpetually before Yehovah.

For us, trimming the wick represents removing what is burned out or corrupted in our lives, while replenishing the oil represents seeking a fresh filling of the Spirit. If we allow sin, complacency, or pride to build up like charred wick, our light smolders and clouds the room instead of shining. Repentance and renewal through the Spirit's oil keep our flame bright and effective for service.

Yeshua later warned the assemblies in Revelation that neglecting their devotion could result in their lampstand being removed (Revelation 2:5). This was not a random image. He was referring

26

back to the menorah of the Temple, the very symbol of His abiding presence among His people. The warning is clear: if the flame is not tended through repentance, obedience, and love, the light will be taken away.

The assembly in **Ephesus** was in danger because they had abandoned their first love. Their works continued, but their passion for Yeshua had faded. Like a wick that has burned too long without being trimmed, their light was dimming. Without repentance, their lampstand would be removed.

The assembly in **Sardis** was warned that though they had a reputation of being alive, they were spiritually dead. Their lampstand was in jeopardy because their flame was little more than smoke, untended and weak.

The assembly in **Laodicea** was lukewarm, neither hot nor cold. They were self - satisfied, yet spiritually empty. Their light was in danger of being extinguished because they relied on themselves instead of the Spirit's oil.

These warnings show that the threat to the lampstands was not about persecution from the outside but neglect on the inside. The danger was spiritual complacency, compromise, and coldness of heart.

For us, the application is direct. The flame of the Spirit within us must be carefully guarded. If our love for Yeshua grows cold, if our walk becomes mechanical, or if our dependence shifts to ourselves, our light will fade. Just as the priests had to trim the wicks and refill the oil every day, we must repent daily, renew our devotion, and keep the fire of the Spirit alive through prayer, the Word, and worship.

A Continual Flame in the Holy Place

The command was clear: the light must never go out. Darkness had no place in the sanctuary. The continual flame spoke of Yehovah's unceasing presence and His eternal covenant with Israel. Just as the fire on the altar outside was never to be extinguished, so the light inside the Holy Place was never to fail.

For us, this means that devotion to Yehovah is not seasonal or occasional. It is daily and continual. If we allow our fire to burn only on Sabbaths or feast days, it will fade in the long stretches of ordinary life. The Spirit calls us to a steady flame, a faith that shines with constancy no matter the season.

The Menorah and the Seven Feasts of Yehovah

The menorah's seven branches also point prophetically to the seven appointed feasts of Yehovah (Leviticus 23). These moedim, or appointed times, form the rhythm of Israel's worship and also illuminate the full plan of redemption in Messiah. Just as the menorah's light guided the priest within the Holy Place, so the feasts are a light for our journey of faith.

1. **Passover (Pesach)** - The first light reminds us of deliverance through the blood of the Lamb. Yeshua is our Passover sacrifice, whose death redeems us from sin.

2. **Unleavened Bread (Chag HaMatzot)** - The second light represents holiness and separation from sin. Yeshua was buried without corruption, and we are called to walk in purity.

28

3. **Firstfruits (Yom HaBikkurim)** - The third light proclaims resurrection. Yeshua rose as the firstfruits of those who sleep, the guarantee of our eternal life.

4. **Pentecost (Shavuot)** - The central shaft of the menorah, from which the other branches extend, aligns with Shavuot. Here, Yehovah gave both the Torah at Sinai and later the outpouring of the Spirit in Acts 2. Yeshua is the Living Word, and by His Spirit the Word is written on our hearts.

The Final Three Feasts: Prophetic Timeline Yet to Come

The spring feasts have already found their fulfillment in Yeshua's death, burial, resurrection, and the giving of the Spirit. The fall feasts, however, point us forward. They serve as prophetic markers of what is still to unfold in God's plan of redemption.

5. **Trumpets (Yom Teruah)** - This feast foreshadows the return of Messiah. Paul writes that the trumpet of God will sound, the dead in Messiah will rise, and we who remain will be gathered to Him (1 Thessalonians 4:16-17). Yeshua Himself spoke of the great trumpet that will signal His gathering of the elect (Matthew 24:31). For us, this means living with readiness, always prepared for the sound that will change history in a moment.

6. **Day of Atonement (Yom Kippur)** - This feast points to a future day of judgment and national cleansing for Israel. Zechariah prophesied that Israel will look upon the One they have pierced and mourn (Zechariah 12:10). It is the day when every account is settled, and Yeshua as High Priest will complete His atoning work on a worldwide scale. For us, it means living in humility, covered by His blood, and soberly awaiting the day when every knee bows before Him.

7.   **Tabernacles (Sukkot)** - The final feast reveals the end of the story: God dwelling with His people. Revelation 21 echoes this feast when it declares, "Behold, the dwelling place of God is with man." Sukkot points to the Messianic Kingdom, when Yeshua reigns, Israel is restored, and all nations come up to worship the King (Zechariah 14:16). For us, it is the hope that one day His presence will be our eternal light and our everlasting joy.

The menorah, therefore, is not only a symbol of God's presence in the sanctuary but also a prophetic timeline of redemption. It shines forward to Messiah's work past, present, and future and reminds us that His Word and His appointed times are a lamp to our feet and a light to our path (Psalm 119:105).

Messiah - Life Parallel: The Light of the Spirit in Us

The menorah's flame finds its ultimate fulfillment in Messiah. Yeshua declared, "I am the light of the world. Whoever follows Me will not walk in darkness, but will have the light of life" (John 8:12). Revelation describes Him walking among the lampstands, which are the assemblies of His people (Revelation 1:12-13, 20). The menorah pointed to Him, the true Light who shines in the darkness.

Yet Yeshua also declared, "You are the light of the world" (Matthew 5:14). Through His Spirit, He places within us the flame of His presence. Like the priests of old, we have a duty to tend this flame. Prayer replenishes the oil. The Word trims the wick, cutting away what is charred and unclean. Worship fans the flame to burn brightly. Without these, the light sputters.

Paul exhorted Timothy, "Fan into flame the gift of God, which is in you" (2 Timothy 1:6). The Spirit's presence is not a one - time experience but a continual fire that must be nourished. The menorah teaches us that yesterday's oil is not enough for today. Daily devotion keeps the lamp of our lives burning steadily before Yehovah.

Teaching Takeaways

- Without the menorah's light, the priests could not see to walk or serve. Without the Spirit's light, we cannot see where to go or how to serve in Messiah.

- The menorah's design with almond blossoms signified life, fruitfulness, and God's watchfulness. Our lives are called to bear fruit and remain spiritually awake.

- Trimming the wicks and replenishing the oil shows that holiness requires daily repentance and continual renewal by the Spirit. Yesterday's oil is not enough for today.

- Yeshua's words in Revelation reveal that lampstands are in jeopardy when devotion fades. Losing first love, becoming lukewarm, or having only the appearance of life places us in danger of losing His light.

- The continual flame in the Holy Place points to God's abiding presence. Our devotion must be steady and constant, not seasonal or occasional.

- The seven branches of the menorah correspond to the seven feasts of Yehovah. The spring feasts reveal what

Messiah has accomplished, while the fall feasts form a prophetic timeline yet to be fulfilled.

- Priests were tasked with helping Israel prepare for the feasts. In Messiah, we are called to prepare our brothers, sisters, and neighbors for the future fulfillment of these moedim.

Reflections for the Reader

- Do you recognize that without the light of the Spirit, you cannot see clearly where to walk or how to serve? How does this shape your daily dependence on Him?

- What "charred wicks" in your life need trimming? Are there sins, habits, or distractions that cloud your flame instead of letting it burn cleanly?

- Yeshua warned Ephesus about losing first love, Sardis about spiritual death, and Laodicea about lukewarmness. Which of these warnings speaks most to you today, and what repentance is He calling you to?

- Is your devotion to Yehovah steady and continual, or is your flame strongest only on certain days or seasons? How can you cultivate a consistent daily walk?

- How do the seven feasts help you understand both what Messiah has already done and what is still to come?

- Priests prepared Israel for the moedim. What practical steps can you take to prepare your family, friends, or community for the future fulfillment of Messiah's return, judgment, and Kingdom?

How to Walk This Out Practically

- **Start your day by trimming.** Ask the Spirit to show you anything in your heart that needs to be cut away so your light burns pure.

- **End your day by replenishing.** Spend time in the Word and prayer before sleep, pouring in fresh oil so the flame does not fade.

- **Honor the feasts.** Learn, rehearse, and celebrate Yah's moedim as prophetic markers of Messiah's redemption. Use them to prepare yourself and to help prepare others.

- **Stay sensitive.** Do not ignore conviction. If the Spirit points to compromise, deal with it quickly before the flame is dimmed.

- **Guard community light.** Encourage your congregation or family to keep their lamps burning. Sometimes trimming and replenishing requires others to walk with us.

- **Look ahead.** Live each day with awareness of the prophetic feasts yet to be fulfilled, walking in readiness for Messiah's return.

Prayer Activation

Father Yehovah, I thank You for the light of the menorah and what it teaches me about Your presence, Your watchfulness, and Your faithfulness. Shine Your light in my heart so that I may see clearly where to walk and how to serve You as a priest in Messiah. Trim away the charred wicks of sin, complacency, and pride, and fill me with fresh oil of Your Spirit each day. Keep me from the errors of Ephesus, Sardis, and Laodicea. Restore me to my first love, awaken me to true life, and make me burn with zeal for You.

Teach me to live with constancy, not letting my flame flicker with seasons, but to burn steadily before You at all times. Help me to see the fullness of redemption revealed in Your feasts and to prepare myself and others for the return of Yeshua, the day of judgment, and the joy of Your Kingdom. May my life be a living menorah, shining with Your light into the darkness. In the name of Yeshua, the true Light, Amen.

Chapter 4: The Bread of the Presence

Inside the Holy Place, opposite the menorah, stood the Table of Showbread. Upon it rested the *Lechem haPanim*, literally "bread of the faces" or "bread of the Presence" (Leviticus 24:5 - 9). This bread was not ordinary food. It symbolized the continual covenant between Yehovah and Israel, a visible reminder that His face and His presence were turned toward His people. Just as the menorah brought light into the sanctuary, so the bread brought fellowship and sustenance into the holy space.

Without the bread, the table was bare. Without Messiah, the Living Bread, our souls are empty.

Baking and Setting Out the Bread Weekly

Every week the priests baked twelve loaves of fine flour, representing the twelve tribes of Israel. These loaves were placed in two rows on the golden table, with **pure frankincense** set beside them as a memorial portion (Leviticus 24:7). The bread was always before Yehovah, a perpetual sign of His covenant with His people.

For the priests, this was a sacred duty. The bread had to be prepared, baked, and set out fresh each week. It could not be stale or neglected. In the same way, our service to Yehovah cannot be half - hearted or offered with leftovers. He deserves our best, our first, and our fresh devotion.

The ingredients of the showbread point us to Messiah and to the life we are called to live in Him. Yeshua is the Bread of Life, not only in the final loaf but in each ingredient that went into its making:

- **The finest flour** - Only the best flour was used, finely ground and pure. This points to the perfection of Yeshua's life and to the fruit of the Spirit that must be cultivated in us: love, joy, peace, patience, kindness, goodness, faithfulness, gentleness, and self - control. We too are to be refined, sifted, and made ready for His use.

- **Pure, clean water** - Water represents both the Word of God and the Spirit. Yeshua is the Living Water, and He washes us with the water of the Word. Our lives must be saturated with His Word if we are to become a reflection of Him.

- **The best oil** - The oil used in the bread and for the menorah came from beaten olives, not crushed by machinery but pressed by hand. This points to the anointing of the Spirit that flows through suffering, endurance, and yieldedness. Yeshua was pressed in Gethsemane, the olive press, and we too are called to let the Spirit produce His fragrance through our surrendered lives.

- **Salt** - Every offering was to be seasoned with salt (Leviticus 2:13). Salt preserves, flavors, and symbolizes covenant faithfulness. Yeshua declared, "You are the salt of the earth" (Matthew 5:13). Our lives are meant to flavor the world with His presence and preserve it from corruption.

- **Frankincense** - The bread was accompanied by pure frankincense as a memorial offering to Yehovah. Frankincense represents prayer and worship, rising as a pleasing aroma before God (Psalm 141:2; Revelation 5:8). The bread was not complete without it, reminding us that our daily walk must not only consist of doing and serving, but also of lifting our lives in prayer and worship. Without the fragrance of devotion, our offering becomes an empty ritual.

The showbread was not merely food; it was an act of worship. In the same way, our lives are not only about producing fruit but also about offering up a continual fragrance of prayer, thanksgiving, and adoration. Just as frankincense filled the sanctuary with a sweet aroma, our prayers rise before Yehovah, completing the offering of our lives.

Salt and Gypsum: A Warning

In Yeshua's day, salt was mined around the Dead Sea. At times it was mixed with **gypsum**, a chalky mineral that looked identical to salt but had no flavor. Salt mixed with gypsum lost its saltiness and could not fulfill its purpose. Yeshua warned, "If the salt loses its taste, how shall its saltiness be restored? It is no longer good for anything except to be thrown out and trampled under people's feet" (Matthew 5:13).

Archaeologists and historians note that gypsum - tainted salt was mixed with water to form a plaster - like paste that was then spread across flat rooftop patios. These rooftops became common places for gatherings and feasts, and the plastered salt was literally trampled underfoot.

This is a powerful picture for us. Gypsum represents the world. It looks similar to true salt, but it is lifeless, bland, and empty. If we as the salt of the earth become mixed with the ways of the world, our witness is diluted, our flavor lost. Instead of being a preservative of life and truth, we become useless, fit only to be cast out and walked upon.

The showbread teaches us not only about Yeshua as the Bread of Life but also about our calling to reflect Him in every ingredient of our lives. We are to be refined like flour, filled with the Word and Spirit like water and oil, seasoned with the salt of covenant faithfulness, and offered up with the fragrance of prayer and worship. If the gypsum of the world enters in, our testimony fades. But if we remain pure, we become bread that nourishes others with His presence.

Replacing the Bread Every Shabbat

Each Sabbath, the priests replaced the bread with new loaves. The old bread, still holy, was eaten by Aaron and his sons in the Holy Place (Leviticus 24:9). Nothing was wasted. What was offered to Yehovah became nourishment for His priests.

Jewish tradition records that the bread did not spoil or mold during the week it sat on the Table of the Presence. Even more, when the priests ate it the following Sabbath, it was as fresh as the day it was baked. This miracle reminded Israel that Yehovah Himself sustained the bread of His presence. He was the One who kept it from corruption.

For us, this teaches several important truths:

- **God's provision does not decay.** Just as the bread remained fresh, the Word of God and the promises of Messiah never grow stale. What He has spoken remains living and active, ready to nourish us.

- **Holiness preserves.** Because the bread was set apart for Yehovah, it was preserved by His power. When we live consecrated lives, His Spirit keeps us from the corruption of the world.

- **True fellowship is sustaining.** The priests ate the holy bread together in the Presence. In the same way, our fellowship in Messiah is not empty ritual but real nourishment that strengthens us week by week.

- **Messiah is incorruptible.** Yeshua, the Bread of Life, did not see decay in the grave (Acts 2:27). He is the living bread that remains eternally fresh, giving life to all who partake of Him.

For our daily walk, this means that what God gives us is not temporary or fragile. His Word is not stale, His Spirit does not spoil, and His fellowship is never empty. If we are faithful to come to His table, He will continually renew and sustain us.

Messiah, the Bread of Life

Yeshua declared, "I am the living bread that came down from heaven. If anyone eats of this bread, he will live forever" (John 6:51). Just as Israel lived by the bread of the Presence set continually before Yehovah, so we live by Messiah, the true Bread of the Presence, who brings us into communion with the Father.

The twelve loaves represented all Israel. Likewise, Yeshua is the Bread given for the life of the whole world. To partake of Him is to receive eternal sustenance, strength for the journey, and fellowship with God.

Yet Paul issued a sobering warning to the Corinthians about eating and drinking of Messiah in an unworthy manner. He wrote that those who failed to discern the body of the Lord were bringing judgment on themselves, which had led to weakness, sickness, and even premature death among them (1 Corinthians 11:27-30).

What Does It Mean to "Fail to Discern the Body of the Lord"?

To fail to discern means to take lightly what is holy. The Corinthians were treating the Lord's Supper as common food and drink. Some were eating to excess while others went hungry, and divisions among them showed that they were not honoring Messiah or His body, the community of believers. In doing so, they treated what was sacred as ordinary and failed to recognize the weight of what the bread and cup represented.

To discern the body of the Lord means at least three things:

1. **Recognizing Messiah's sacrifice** - The bread represents His body broken for us, and the cup represents His blood poured out. To eat and drink without gratitude, repentance, and reverence is to dishonor His offering.

2. **Recognizing the holiness of fellowship** - The body of the Lord also refers to His people, the congregation of believers. When we harbor bitterness, division, or selfishness, and yet partake of communion, we are failing to discern His body as sacred and unified.

3. **Recognizing our call to holiness** - Partaking is not only a memorial of what He has done, but also a call to live set apart as His body in the world. To eat unworthily is to claim fellowship with Him while walking in willful disobedience.

How Can I Do This?

For us, this warning means that coming to the Lord's table is never casual. Just as the priests ate the showbread only in a consecrated place, we must approach Messiah with reverence and self-examination. It means:

- Coming with repentance, asking the Spirit to trim away the charred wicks of sin before we partake.

- Coming with gratitude, remembering the price of His broken body and shed blood.

- Coming with reconciliation, seeking unity with our brothers and sisters, since they too are part of His body.

- Coming with obedience, committing to walk in holiness as priests of the Living God.

When we discern the body of the Lord rightly, communion becomes not a ritual but a renewal. It strengthens us, heals us, and unites us with Messiah and with one another. The Bread of the Presence points us to this sacred fellowship, reminding us that Yeshua is incorruptible and holy, and that His presence among us is not to be taken lightly.

Messiah - Life Parallel: Feeding and Presenting the Word

41

The bread was not only for display but for nourishment. In the same way, the Word of God is not for us to admire from afar but to consume, internalize, and share. The priests ate the bread in a holy place, teaching us that fellowship with Messiah is sacred and not to be treated lightly.

The bread of the Presence was always visible in the Holy Place. It was a continual reminder that Yehovah's provision was set before His people, never absent, never withdrawn. In the same way, our lives are meant to be a living witness of His provision. Others should be able to see the evidence of His Word alive in us, just as clearly as the priest could see the loaves on the golden table.

Eating the bread also symbolized participation in covenant fellowship. The priests were sustained by what was offered to Yehovah. For us, feeding on Messiah means that His life becomes our strength, His Word becomes our nourishment, and His Spirit becomes our sustaining power. When we partake of Him, we are not only filled for ourselves but equipped to carry His life into the world around us.

As priests in Messiah, we are called not only to feed but also to present. The bread was displayed publicly before Yehovah, not hidden away. Likewise, the Word should not remain hidden in our hearts but be shared openly with joy. We are bearers of His presence, and our lives should carry the fragrance and the sustenance of Messiah wherever we go.

Weekly renewal, continual fellowship, and faithful service are the lessons of the showbread. It calls us to come often to the table of Messiah, to be filled deeply with His life, and then to go forth as living bread that nourishes the people around us.

Teaching Takeaways

- The Bread of the Presence symbolized covenant fellowship between Yehovah and His people. Without it, the table was bare. Without Messiah, our lives are empty.

- The ingredients of the showbread each point to Messiah and to our walk in Him: fine flour (fruit of the Spirit), water (Word and Spirit), oil (Spirit's anointing through surrender), salt (covenant faithfulness), and frankincense (prayer and worship).

- Gypsum looked like salt but had no flavor. If we mix with the world's lifeless ways, we lose our saltiness and our witness.

- The priests prepared twelve fresh loaves every week, reminding us that devotion and service to Yehovah must be fresh, not stale or leftover.

- Each Sabbath the bread was renewed, teaching us the importance of weekly fellowship, rest, and renewal in Messiah.

- The miracle of the bread not molding showed that God Himself sustains His provision. His Word never grows stale, His Spirit never spoils, and Messiah is incorruptible.

- Paul's warning in 1 Corinthians 11 shows that to partake of Messiah wrongly is dangerous. To "fail to discern the body of the Lord" means to treat His sacrifice, His people, and our call to holiness as ordinary.

- Communion, like the showbread, is sacred. To discern the body rightly is to come with repentance, gratitude, unity, and obedience. When we do, Messiah nourishes us with life, health, and strength.

- The bread was always visible on the golden table, reminding us that our lives too must be a visible testimony of God's provision. Others should be able to see His Word alive in us.

- Yeshua is the Bread of Life, the true Bread of the Presence, who sustains us and brings us into eternal fellowship with the Father.

Reflections for the Reader

- How do you prepare yourself to "set out fresh bread" before Yehovah each week? Is your devotion to Him offered with freshness and intention, or with leftovers?

- In what ways do you experience Shabbat or weekly fellowship as a time of renewal and nourishment?

- Do you regularly feed on the Bread of Life through His Word and Spirit, or are you trying to survive on yesterday's manna?

- Where might gypsum be mixing into your saltiness, diluting your witness and leaving your life bland? What would it look like to remove it?

- Do you believe that God's provision for you is incorruptible, that His Word never grows stale, and that His Spirit always sustains? How does that change your confidence in daily life?

- Is your walk balanced with both bread and frankincense - feeding on the Word and lifting your life as prayer and worship? How can you grow in both?

- Before you come to the Lord's table, do you pause to discern His body? Are you remembering His sacrifice with gratitude, reconciling with others in unity, and committing to walk in holiness? Or are you treating communion as routine?

- Is your life a visible witness of the Bread of Life? Do those around you see the nourishment of His Word at work in you?

How to Walk This Out Practically

- **Feed daily.** Set aside consistent time to read, study, and meditate on Scripture. Do not wait for Sabbath or Sunday alone - keep the bread fresh in your life.

- **Examine yourself.** Before taking communion or leading others, pause to repent and ensure your heart is clean before Yehovah.

- **Stay salty.** Refuse to let compromise dilute your witness. Guard against the gypsum of worldly influence that robs you of spiritual effectiveness.

- **Offer fragrance.** Let trials press you into deeper prayer and worship. See your hardships as the crushing that releases a sweet aroma to God.

- **Feed others.** Share what you are learning with family, friends, or your congregation. Remember: priests were responsible to present the bread, not only eat it.

- **Guard unity.** Discern the body of Messiah. Choose to forgive, to reconcile, and to honor others in the community of faith.

Prayer Activation

Father Yehovah, thank You for the Bread of the Presence that pointed to Yeshua, the true Bread of Life. I ask that You make me hungry for Your Word and faithful to prepare fresh devotion before You each day. Refine me like flour, wash me with the water of the Word, anoint me with the oil of Your Spirit, and season me with the salt of covenant faithfulness. Add to my life the fragrance of frankincense, the aroma of prayer and worship rising continually before You. Keep me from the blandness of gypsum, and let my life retain the flavor of Your presence.

Thank You that Your provision never decays. Your Word is always fresh, Your Spirit never spoils, and Messiah is incorruptible. Renew me each week as I come into Your presence, and let me never treat lightly the fellowship You have given me through Messiah. Help me to discern the body of the Lord rightly. Let me remember His sacrifice with reverence, approach Your table with repentance and gratitude, seek unity with my brothers and sisters, and commit to walk in holiness.

Make my life a visible testimony of Your provision, like bread set openly on the table. Let others see in me the nourishment of Your Word, the fragrance of prayer, and the strength of Your Spirit. Feed my soul with the living bread that comes down from heaven, and teach me to share it with my family, friends, and neighbors so that they too may taste and see that You are good. In the name of Yeshua, the Bread of the Presence, Amen.

Chapter 5: Teaching and Judging

The priestly service did not stop at the altar, lampstand, or table. Much of the Levites' calling was lived out among the people, in the villages and cities of Israel. They were not only ministers of worship but also teachers of Torah and judges of disputes. Their task was to make known the ways of Yehovah so that Israel would walk in holiness, distinguish between clean and unclean, and live in righteousness before God.

This priestly duty reveals the centrality of God's Word in daily life. Without teaching, the people would stumble. Without discernment, confusion would reign. Without judgment, justice would collapse. The priesthood was designed to keep Israel aligned with Yehovah's covenant in both worship and daily conduct.

Teaching Torah to Israel

Leviticus 10:10-11 commands the priests to distinguish between holy and common, and to teach Israel all the statutes of Yehovah. Deuteronomy 33:10 says of Levi, "They shall teach Jacob Your judgments, and Israel Your law." The priests were not free to invent their own opinions or traditions. They were charged with passing on exactly what Yehovah had spoken, nothing more and nothing less.

Most Levites did not serve daily in the Tabernacle or later in the Temple. Their service took place among the people, in villages and cities throughout the land. Their lives were lived in close proximity to their neighbors, and their primary work was to teach and preserve the knowledge of Yehovah among His people. Every day brought opportunities to explain the Torah, answer questions, and guide the people in righteousness.

This is at the heart of priesthood, and it is at the heart of our calling in Messiah. Priestly ministry is not confined to sacred buildings or special gatherings. It is lived out in daily life, in conversations at the table, in counsel during conflict, in teaching children, and in mentoring others in the way of truth.

Are you prepared to teach? If someone asked you right now to explain the foundations of our faith, could you? The writer of Hebrews challenges us in this very area:

"Therefore let us leave the elementary doctrine of Messiah and go on to maturity, not laying again a foundation of repentance from dead works and of faith toward God, and of instruction about baptisms, the laying on of hands, the resurrection of the dead, and eternal judgment" (Hebrews 6:1-2).

These six elementary doctrines are the milk of the Word, the bread every believer must know and be able to share. Yet each of them contains a depth most believers have never studied carefully:

1. **Repentance from dead works** - Repentance (*teshuvah, metanoia*) is more than saying sorry. It is a complete turning back to God and away from sin. Dead works are sins - lifeless deeds that lead to death. Repentance means turning from lawlessness and realigning with Torah. From Genesis to Revelation, Yehovah repeats this same truth in different ways: "If you love Me, keep My commandments."

2. **Faith toward God** - Faith (*emunah, pistis*) is not just mental belief but relational trust that leads to obedience. It operates as a spiritual law and moves through hearing, believing, confessing, and acting. Fear and doubt constantly war against faith, which must be guarded in our thought life.

3. **Instruction about baptisms (immersions)** - Immersion (*mikvah*) was common in Hebrew life, tied to ritual purity, covenant, and transition. The New Covenant reveals at least three major immersions: water (identification with Messiah), blood (cleansing of the conscience), and Spirit (empowerment to walk in holiness). Yet these three are not even the full list of immersions found in Scripture. Other examples include immersion into the cloud and into Moses (1 Corinthians 10:2), immersion into fire (Matthew 3:11), immersion into suffering (Mark 10:38-39), and immersion into the Body of Messiah (1 Corinthians 12:13). Together, these show that immersion is not only a ritual once in life, but an ongoing picture of living continually immersed in Him.

4. **Laying on of hands** - Found throughout Scripture in blessing, ordination, sacrifice, impartation of the Spirit, and healing. This practice is not casual but sacred. It represents transference, commissioning, and spiritual impartation under the guidance of the Spirit.

5. **Resurrection of the dead** - Taught in Isaiah and Daniel long before Yeshua declared, "I am the resurrection and the life." Believers will be raised with glorified bodies, while all humanity will face resurrection - either to eternal life or eternal separation.

6. **Eternal judgment** - The final judgment is certain and eternal. Books will be opened: the Book of Life, the Book of Remembrance, and the records of works. Judgment belongs to Yeshua, who spares His own from wrath but will bring everlasting separation upon those who reject Him.

If these foundations are not solid, how can we build a life of maturity? Just as the Levites were charged with teaching Israel the Torah in every generation, we too are responsible to pass on the truths of Messiah with clarity. These six doctrines are meant to be elementary, yet without them firmly established we cannot grow into maturity or help others do the same. The question is not only whether you understand them, but whether you are prepared to teach them to others.

Distinguishing Between Holy and Profane

Another priestly responsibility was discernment. They had to know what was clean and unclean, holy and profane, and then help the people apply those distinctions. This was not merely about ritual purity. It was about living with sensitivity to Yehovah's presence in every aspect of life.

Holiness means separation unto God. The priest taught Israel that not everything is acceptable, and not everything is equal. Some things are consecrated for worship, while others defile. Some ways lead to life, while others lead to death. Discernment is the backbone of holiness.

For us in Messiah, this means cultivating spiritual discernment by the Spirit and the Word. We are called to test everything, to hold fast to what is good, and to abstain from every form of evil (1 Thessalonians 5:21-22). Without discernment, the light of the menorah grows dim and the bread of the Word is mishandled.

Serving as Judges in Disputes

51

The priests also served as judges when conflicts arose. Deuteronomy 17:8-11 describes how difficult cases were brought before the priests, who would seek Yehovah's judgment and then render a decision. Their role was to establish justice by God's standards, not by human preference.

This shows us that righteousness is not only personal but also communal. A holy people must be guided by holy judgment. Justice in Israel was rooted in Torah, administered by priests who were accountable to God. In this way, disputes were settled, peace was restored, and the covenant community was preserved.

In our day, one of the most quoted verses from unbelievers and even some believers is Yeshua's statement, "Do not judge, or you too will be judged" (Matthew 7:1). Many use this as a blanket prohibition against discernment or correction. But taken in context, Yeshua was warning against hypocritical judgment - pointing out the speck in your brother's eye while ignoring the plank in your own. He was not forbidding righteous judgment but exposing self-righteousness and hypocrisy.

Elsewhere, Scripture makes it clear that judgment - in the sense of discernment and application of God's Word - is a vital part of spiritual maturity. Paul says, "The spiritual man judges all things, but is himself to be judged by no one" (1 Corinthians 2:15). To judge rightly is to weigh, discern, and evaluate all things through the lens of God's Word and Spirit. Yeshua Himself commands in John 7:24, "Do not judge by appearances, but judge with right judgment."

For us, judging does not mean condemning with arrogance. It means applying God's Word in love and truth, correcting sin, and guiding others toward righteousness. Paul reminded the

Corinthians that believers must not tolerate unrepentant sin but restore one another in humility (Galatians 6:1; 1 Corinthians 5:12-13). To refuse to judge at all is not compassion but negligence, leaving others in danger of continuing down destructive paths.

This failure to judge rightly is one of the reasons our culture is in its current state. People try to redefine love as unconditional approval, removing correction from its definition. Yet Scripture shows that love and correction are inseparable. To love without truth is not biblical love but permissiveness. God is indeed love (1 John 4:8), but He is also a consuming fire, a jealous God, a righteous Judge who does not change. He clearly declares what He loves and what He hates (Proverbs 6:16-19). To proclaim His love while ignoring His holiness is to present a false god of our own making.

Messiah - Life Parallel: Discipleship and Guidance

Yeshua is our High Priest, the perfect Teacher and Judge. He taught His disciples the Torah of the Kingdom, He distinguished between holy and profane, and He will one day judge the nations in righteousness. As His body, we are called to reflect these same functions.

To teach is to disciple, to pass on His Word to others with clarity and faithfulness. To discern is to walk in holiness, guarding our hearts and guiding others away from compromise. To judge is to correct in love, to call out sin when necessary, and to point people back to the path of righteousness.

This priestly calling continues through us as we live among our neighbors, family, and congregations. Most of our ministry will not take place inside a sanctuary but in the daily moments of life. Every

53

conversation, every decision, every act of discernment is an opportunity to bring the Word of God to bear. The question is not whether you are teaching, discerning, or judging - the question is whether you are doing so faithfully.

Teaching Takeaways

- The priest's role extended beyond the Tabernacle. They lived among the people as teachers, guides, and judges.

- Priests were commanded to teach Israel the Torah as it was given, without adding or subtracting. True teaching means faithfully transmitting God's truth.

- The six elementary doctrines in Hebrews 6:1-2 are the foundations of our faith: repentance, faith, baptisms, laying on of hands, resurrection, and eternal judgment. These are meant to be "elementary," yet many believers have never studied them deeply.

- Holiness requires discernment. To distinguish between holy and profane, clean and unclean, is the foundation of walking with Yehovah.

- Priests also judged disputes, showing that justice is rooted in God's Word, not human opinion.

- "Do not judge" is one of the most misused verses today. Scripture calls us not to hypocritical judgment, but to righteous judgment rooted in truth and humility.

- Yeshua is our perfect Teacher and Judge. As His priests, we are called to disciple others, guide them in holiness, and lovingly correct with truth.

- Most priestly ministry takes place outside the sanctuary, in daily life. The same is true for us - our witness is lived out in our homes, neighborhoods, and communities.

Reflections for the Reader

- Could you clearly explain the six elementary doctrines to someone else - repentance, faith, baptisms, laying on of hands, resurrection, and eternal judgment? Which ones do you need to study more deeply?

- In your daily choices, how do you practice discernment between what is holy and what is profane?

- When conflict arises, do you apply God's Word with humility and truth, or do you lean on personal preference?

- Have you avoided judging others out of fear of conflict or criticism? How can you learn to judge with righteous judgment as Scripture commands?

- Do you tend to equate love with approval? How does God's unchanging holiness reshape your understanding of true love?

- Do you see your daily interactions with neighbors, coworkers, and family as opportunities for priestly ministry?

How to Walk This Out Practically

- **Revisit the basics.** Study Hebrews 6:1-2 and make sure you understand and can teach the elementary doctrines. Practice explaining them to your family or small group.

- **Discern daily.** Ask, "Is this holy or profane? Clean or unclean?" Let this question guide choices in entertainment, relationships, and lifestyle.

- **Judge rightly.** When confronted with sin - in your own life or others - address it with love and truth instead of silence or harshness.

- **Anchor in the Word.** Use Scripture, not personal opinion, as the standard for teaching and correction.

- **Mentor others.** Take responsibility for someone younger in the faith. Walk with them, answer their questions, and guide them in righteousness.

- **Balance love and truth.** Remember Yehovah is both merciful and righteous. Aim to reflect both in your teaching, discernment, and correction.

Prayer Activation

Father Yehovah, thank You for calling me into the priesthood of Messiah. Help me to be faithful in teaching Your Word, not adding to it or taking away from it, but delivering it with clarity and love. Strengthen me to know the elementary doctrines and to be ready to share them with others.

Give me discernment to distinguish between what is holy and what is profane, and courage to guide others with truth. Teach me to judge with righteousness, not from pride or appearance, but with humility and obedience to Your Word. Guard me from hypocrisy, and let my judgments be rooted in love and truth.

Father, I repent for the times I have been silent when I should have spoken, or when I confused love with approval. Help me to reflect Your love rightly - a love that corrects, restores, and calls us to holiness. Remind me that You are not only love, but also jealous, righteous, and unchanging, hating what is evil and delighting in what is good.

Yeshua, You are the perfect Teacher and Judge. Conform me to Your image so that I may disciple others, mentor in love, and guide those around me into Your righteousness. Let my life be a visible testimony of Your wisdom, justice, and mercy. In Your holy name, Amen.

Chapter 6: Feast Observance and Leadership

The priesthood was never meant to exist for itself. It existed to lead the people of Israel into the appointed times (*moedim*), the holy convocations when Yehovah gathered His people to remember, to worship, and to rehearse His redemptive plan. Priests were not only guardians of holiness in the daily service but leaders of worship in the great assemblies. They carried visible and audible responsibilities - from presenting sacrifices during the Feasts, to sounding the trumpets that called the nation together, to bearing the Ark of the Covenant in sacred procession.

Each act was a prophetic shadow, pointing forward to Messiah. And in Him, each finds its fulfillment.

Leading Sacrifices and Rituals During the Feasts

Numbers 28 - 29 lays out the extensive priestly duties for each Feast of Yehovah. These offerings were not casual additions to daily life but central acts of worship. During Passover, Pentecost, and Tabernacles, the priests led the people in presenting sacrifices that rehearsed the story of redemption. The blood of bulls and goats could not take away sin, but they pointed forward to the perfect sacrifice of Messiah (Hebrews 10:1-4).

In Chapter 3, we saw how the menorah pictured the seven Feasts of Yehovah as a light to our path, each feast revealing a stage in God's redemptive plan. The spring Feasts have already been fulfilled in Messiah's first coming - Passover in His death, Firstfruits in His resurrection, and Pentecost in the outpouring of the Spirit.

The fall Feasts remain prophetic of His return - the trumpet call announcing His coming, the Day of Atonement pointing to His judgment and mercy, and Tabernacles picturing His dwelling among us.

But the priestly responsibility did not end with knowing these truths - they were called to *lead the people in celebrating them*. They guided the nation step by step through the moedim, ensuring that Israel did not just hear about the Feasts but actually participated in them.

In the same way, we as priests in Messiah are called not only to understand the Feasts prophetically but also to walk others through them practically. These appointed times are rehearsals of Messiah's work and reminders of His covenant faithfulness. By leading our families, congregations, and communities in celebrating them, we point back to His finished work, experience His presence now, and look forward to His return.

Blowing Trumpets for Convocations

Numbers 10:8 - 10 commands the sons of Aaron to blow the silver trumpets over burnt offerings and peace offerings, and to sound them for convocations. These blasts marked days of gladness, Feasts, and appointed times. The trumpet was both a call and a reminder - a call to gather, and a reminder that Yehovah was with His people.

The trumpet was also a sound of watchfulness and repentance. Its blasts signaled war, warned of danger, and called the nation to awaken from slumber. The Feast of Trumpets, in particular, prepared Israel for the solemn days leading to Atonement. It was not only about joy but also about readiness - a people stirred to repent and prepare to meet their God.

For us, the trumpet still carries prophetic weight. Paul ties the return of Messiah to the last trumpet (1 Corinthians 15:52; 1 Thessalonians 4:16). The sound that once gathered Israel will one day summon the nations and raise the dead. Until then, we are called to live as those who hear the trumpet now - awake, alert, repentant, and ready. Priestly leadership with the trumpet foreshadowed the ultimate gathering of God's people in resurrection and glory, but it also challenges us to sound the alarm today: to call people to turn back, to wake up, and to prepare for Messiah's coming.

Carrying the Ark in Processions

When Israel crossed the Jordan, it was the priests who bore the Ark on their shoulders (Joshua 3:3 - 6). They went ahead of the people, stepping into the waters before the nation followed. The Ark represented the throne of Yehovah, His covenant presence among His people. To carry the Ark was to bear His throne, His name, and His authority.

This reminds us that leadership in God's kingdom is not about position but about carrying His presence. Priestly leadership always went before the people, not for prestige, but to make a way for others to enter into the promises of God. Messiah is the greater Ark-bearer, going before us into death and resurrection so that we may follow Him into life.

As priests in Messiah, we too are called to carry His presence into the world. Paul says, "We are ambassadors for Messiah, God making His appeal through us" (2 Corinthians 5:20). An ambassador does not represent himself but the kingdom that sent him. In the same way, when we walk as priests, we bear the authority, presence, and message of the Kingdom of Yah.

Carrying His presence means showing forth His reign in our words, our actions, and our relationships. It means that when we step into a workplace, a home, or a community, the presence of the King enters with us. The priests carried the Ark on their shoulders; we carry the Spirit of the living God within us. Just as the Ark went before Israel into the Jordan, we go before others as witnesses of His Kingdom, making a way for them to see, believe, and follow.

Messiah - Life Parallel: Leading in Worship and Unity

Yeshua is revealed in every Feast, every trumpet, and every procession. He is the Lamb of Passover, the Firstfruits of resurrection, the Lord who poured out the Spirit at Pentecost, and the coming King who will tabernacle among us. He is the One announced by the trumpet of God, and He is the true Ark who carries us into covenant life.

As priests in Messiah, our calling is to lead others into these appointed times - not through rituals of animals and blood, but through worship that points to Him. We are called to proclaim the moedim as rehearsals of His redemption, to guide others in celebrating them, to gather God's people in unity, and to carry His presence into every place we go.

Leadership in the kingdom is priestly leadership: pointing beyond ourselves to Messiah, calling the people together, and walking before them with His presence on our shoulders.

Teaching Takeaways

- Priests tied the rhythm of Israel's life to Yehovah's calendar by leading in the Feasts.

- The seven Feasts of Yehovah are prophetic pictures: the spring fulfilled in Messiah's first coming, the fall pointing to His return.

- Priestly leadership meant not only knowing the moedim but guiding the people step by step through them in celebration.

- The trumpet blasts called Israel together, warned of danger, and prepared hearts for repentance. They foreshadow the final trumpet that will raise the dead and summon all nations.

- Carrying the Ark pictured leadership as bearing God's presence before His people. Today, we carry His Spirit within us as ambassadors of His Kingdom.

- True leadership is not about prestige but about presence - bringing the reign of Yah into every space we enter.

- In Messiah, leadership means pointing others to Him, helping them walk through the Feasts, and gathering the people of God in unity under His covenant.

Reflections for the Reader

- Do you see God's calendar as central to your walk with Him, or as optional?

- Could you explain how the seven Feasts of Yehovah point to Messiah's redemptive work, past and future?

- Beyond knowing them, are you prepared to *lead others* through the moedim - your family, your community, your congregation?

- The trumpets summoned Israel to awaken and repent. How are you sounding the alarm in your own circle, calling people to readiness for Messiah's return?

- In what ways are you carrying God's presence into your daily life so that others see His Kingdom through you?

- As an ambassador of Messiah, what message are you presenting about the King you represent?

How to Walk This Out Practically

- **Learn the feasts.** Study each moed, its scriptural foundation, and how it points to Messiah. Don't just read about them - rehearse them in your home and community.

- **Mark the calendar.** Set aside the times Yah calls holy, not only for yourself but as a witness to others. Live by His rhythm, not the world's.

- **Be a trumpet.** Share the message of Messiah's return with boldness. Call others to repentance, readiness, and hope.

- **Create rehearsal spaces.** Help your family or congregation practice the feasts. Teach the story, prepare the meal, explain the symbols.

- **Carry His presence.** Live as an ambassador. Be mindful that wherever you go - work, school, community - you bear the Ark of His presence, and others are watching to follow.

- **Unite around Messiah.** Use the feasts as opportunities not to divide but to unite the people of God in worship, joy, and expectation.

Prayer Activation

Father Yehovah, thank You for the appointed times You set from the beginning, Feasts that reveal Messiah and remind us of Your covenant faithfulness. Teach me not only to know them but to lead others in celebrating them. Make me faithful to walk my family and community through Your moedim, so we may rehearse Messiah's work together and be ready for His return.

Let me hear the sound of Your trumpet and respond with joy and readiness. Use me to call others into unity, repentance, and worship. Make my voice like a trumpet, sounding the alarm for those who are asleep, and preparing hearts for the coming King.

Help me to carry Your presence as the priests carried the Ark - not in pride but in humility, as an ambassador of Your Kingdom. Let me show forth Your reign in my words, my actions, and my relationships, so that when I enter a place, Your presence is seen and felt.

Yeshua, You are the Lamb, the Firstfruits, the Lord of Pentecost, and the coming King who will dwell with us forever. Let every feast I observe, every trumpet I sound, and every step I take carrying Your presence point to You alone. Amen.

Chapter 7: Guarding and Serving in the Temple

From the very beginning, God has called His people to guard. Back in Genesis, Adam was told to work and keep the garden. The Hebrew word for "keep" is *shamar*, which means to watch, to protect, to guard. Adam's job was to keep the garden safe, to protect what God had entrusted to him. But when the serpent came, Adam failed to guard, and the result was exile.

This same theme runs all through Scripture. Guarding is not a side detail. It shows up from Eden to the Temple, and all the way into the New Testament, where we are told to guard our hearts and to guard the faith.

The priests lived this out in a very practical way. Some were stationed at the gates. Others guarded against anyone trying to enter who should not. Still others were responsible for carrying the holy things during times of transport. All of these jobs were a visible reminder that God's presence is holy, and it must be treated with reverence.

And all of this rests on God's own promise: "Yehovah bless you and keep you" (Numbers 6:24). He guards us, and He also calls us to guard what He has given us.

Stationed at Gates and Entrances

1 Chronicles 9:17-27 tells us about the gatekeepers. They had shifts. They held the keys. They opened the doors each morning and closed them each night. They watched over the storehouses and the treasuries.

66

Think about that for a moment. The gates were the first line of protection. Whatever came in shaped the life inside. Whatever was kept out protected the holiness within. Israel learned through the priesthood that holiness has boundaries. It is not vague. It is not open to whoever or whatever wants to walk in. The gatekeepers made those boundaries visible.

Guarding Against Unauthorized Entry

Numbers 3:38 says Moses, Aaron, and the priests were stationed at the east side of the camp to guard the sanctuary and protect Israel from wrath. Why? Because holiness has weight. When it is ignored, harm follows.

Scripture gives us plenty of examples. Nadab and Abihu brought unauthorized fire and died before Yehovah. Korah rebelled and the earth swallowed him and his followers. King Uzziah tried to take priestly duties into his own hands, and leprosy broke out on his forehead. Uzzah reached out to steady the Ark and died instantly because it was not to be touched casually.

These stories are not about God being harsh. They are about the danger of treating His presence as common. Guarding is how love protects what is holy.

Carrying and Caring for Holy Objects

Numbers 4 describes the transport duties. The Kohathites carried the most holy things, but only after Aaron's sons had carefully covered them. The Ark was wrapped and veiled so it could not be seen or touched. The Lampstand, the Table, and the altars were each covered with special cloth. Gershon carried the curtains. Merari carried the frames and pillars. Every group had a role. Every task mattered.

The lesson is clear. You do not drag holy things through life. You cover them. You carry them carefully. You follow God's order.

And when people forgot this, the results were devastating. In 1 Samuel 6, the Philistines returned the Ark on a cart. The men of Beth Shemesh rejoiced to see it, but some made the mistake of looking into the Ark. Scripture says God struck down seventy men because of their irreverence. That Ark contained the testimony, the manna, and Aaron's rod - reminders of covenant. To pry it open was not curiosity; it was desecration. The holy is never to be treated as common.

The Pattern of Guarding in Scripture

This thread runs through the entire Bible. It begins with God Himself. "Yehovah bless you and keep you." He is the Keeper of Israel. He appoints watchmen on the walls who are not to keep silent (Isaiah 62). Ezekiel describes the watchman who must sound the alarm when danger approaches. Nehemiah closed the gates of Jerusalem on the Sabbath to guard the holiness of the day. David prayed, "Set a guard over my mouth." Solomon told his son, "Guard your heart above all else." Paul says the peace of God will guard your heart and mind in Messiah Yeshua.

Do you notice the theme? Guarding is not just about walls and gates. It is about your words, your time, your heart, your community, and your faith.

Messiah - Life Parallel: Guarding Hearts, Protecting the Faith, Stewarding Gifts

In Messiah, this call to guard takes on an even deeper meaning.

1. **Guard your heart.** Proverbs 4:23 says everything in life flows from it. Watch what you let through the gates of your eyes and ears. Philippians 4 promises that the peace of God will act like a garrison over your heart and mind when you pray, give thanks, and fix your thoughts on what is true.

2. **Guard the faith.** Jude tells us to contend for the faith once delivered. Paul told Timothy to guard the good deposit. False teachers creep in unnoticed. Wolves come among the flock. We must hold fast to the trustworthy Word, correcting in love but never lowering the gate to error.

3. **Guard the community.** Yeshua gave us a process for restoration in Matthew 18. Paul told the Corinthians to deal with unrepentant sin for the sake of the person and the body. True love includes correction. To remove correction is to hollow out love.

4. **Guard and steward your gifts.** Paul said not to quench the Spirit, not to despise prophecies, but to test everything. Gifts must be covered by character and accountability. Hunger without holiness is dangerous.

5. **Guard time and rhythms.** The Feasts, Sabbaths, and daily prayers trained Israel to live in God's order. Nehemiah shut the gates on Sabbath. We can shut our digital gates, too. Guard your time so that God's presence shapes your rhythm.

Practicing Gatekeeping in Daily Life

So what does this look like for us today?

- Set watches: begin and end each day with prayer and the Word.

- Post sentries: decide ahead of time what you will not allow into your heart or home.

- Walk your walls: check often for breaches that need repair through repentance or reconciliation.

- Follow transport protocols: treat holy things like prayer, Scripture, and people with care and preparation.

- Use your keys: open wide to the repentant and the hungry, but close firmly to lies and destruction.

Teaching Takeaways

- Guarding runs through Scripture, from Adam in Eden to priests in the Temple.

- God keeps His people, and He calls His people to keep what He entrusts to them.

- Gatekeepers, coverings, and protocols made holiness visible. These were acts of love, not legalism.

- Unauthorized entry harms. Nadab and Abihu, Korah, Uzziah, Uzzah, and the men of Beth Shemesh all show what happens when holiness is treated as common.

- In Messiah, we guard our hearts, the faith, the community, and the gifts. His peace becomes a garrison over us.

- Stewardship of gifts requires holiness, accountability, and humility.

- Gatekeeping is practical. Set watches. Post sentries. Walk your walls. Follow God's order. Use your keys.

Reflections for the Reader

- Where are the open gates in your life right now? Eyes, ears, time, relationships? What sentry needs to return?

- Do you rely on God to keep you while neglecting your own responsibility to guard what He has entrusted to you?

- How do you handle holy things like prayer, Scripture, and fellowship? With reverence, or with casualness?

- The men of Beth Shemesh looked into the Ark and were struck down. Have you treated holy things as common in your life? What would repentance look like?

- Where has "love without correction" weakened your home or fellowship? How can you restore love and truth together this week?

- Are your spiritual gifts covered by accountability and character? Who do you allow to test and strengthen you?

- If God's peace is a garrison, what practices help you remain under His guard every day?

How to Walk This Out Practically

- **Guard your gates.** Pay attention to what you allow through your eyes, ears, and heart. Be intentional about holiness in what you consume and permit.

- **Post watchmen.** Invite trusted brothers or sisters to help keep you accountable in vulnerable areas of your life.

- **Honor the holy.** Handle Scripture, worship, communion, and ministry with reverence, never casually.

- **Protect your home.** Pray over your household regularly, dedicating your family, possessions, and space to Yah's protection.

- **Stand watch in prayer.** Intercede for your congregation, community, and leaders as a spiritual gatekeeper.

- **Carry His presence.** Remember you are an ambassador. Live in such a way that others recognize the holiness of the One you carry.

Prayer Activation

Father Yehovah, thank You that You bless and keep Your people. Place Your Name on me again. Let Your peace guard my heart and mind in Messiah Yeshua.

Teach me to guard what You have entrusted. Set a guard over my mouth. Close the gates to lies, lust, pride, and fear. Open the gates to truth, humility, purity, and faith.

Help me guard the faith with courage and gentleness. Let me hold to Your Word, refute errors in love, and restore the broken with compassion. Give me wisdom to use the keys You have given - wide open to mercy, but firm in holiness.

Stir up the gifts You have placed within me. Clothe them with character and obedience. Let me carry Your presence as a protector of Your Kingdom. Wherever I go, let others encounter Your presence and be moved to honor You as King.

Yeshua, Great High Priest, keep me in Your way, and teach me to keep Your way. Amen.

Chapter 8: Musical Worship and Ministry

When David organized the priesthood and Levites, he established not only gatekeepers, judges, and teachers, but also musicians. Worship was not an afterthought. It was central to life with God. 1 Chronicles 23:5 records that David appointed four thousand Levites to praise Yehovah with instruments he had made. In 1 Chronicles 25, he set apart Asaph, Heman, and Jeduthun to prophesy with lyres, harps, and cymbals. The music of the Temple was not entertainment. It was a priestly service.

Worship, in its truest form, was ministry before Yehovah. When Levites sang and played, they were not performing for the people but ministering to the Lord Himself. They stood before the Ark with instruments and voices lifted, surrounding the presence of God with praise.

Singing Psalms and Playing Instruments Before Yehovah

The psalms we still sing today were birthed out of this priestly ministry. David wrote, "Sing to the Lord a new song" (Psalm 96:1). The Levites carried this command into practice. Their singing and playing was constant - morning and evening, in the Feasts, and in daily service. Music was woven into sacrifice, prayer, and procession.

Their songs were not meant to impress Israel but to glorify Yehovah. In fact, their purpose was to remind Israel that God Himself was enthroned on the praises of His people (Psalm 22:3).

The sound of worship was the atmosphere of His throne room made audible on earth.

This truth is confirmed throughout Scripture. When the prophet Elisha was asked to give a word from the Lord, he said, "Bring me a musician." As the musician played, the hand of Yehovah came upon him and he began to prophesy (2 Kings 3:15). Music became a vessel that opened the way for the Spirit to move in prophetic gifts.

In the New Testament, Paul and Silas were beaten, chained, and thrown into the inner prison. Around midnight they were heard singing hymns and psalms. Their praise rose above the darkness of the dungeon, and suddenly an earthquake shook the foundations of the prison. The doors flew open and their chains fell off. A supernatural intervention was released as they worshiped (Acts 16:25-26).

Both stories show us that worship is more than expression. It is a channel through which the Spirit moves, gifts are activated, and heaven breaks into earth. Singing psalms and playing instruments before Yehovah was not simply about beauty or tradition - it was about ministering to Him in such a way that His presence was welcomed and His power released.

Ministering Before the Ark with Praise

1 Chronicles 16 describes how David appointed Levites to minister before the Ark with thanksgiving and praise. Asaph struck the cymbals. Heman and Jeduthun played harps and lyres. Priests blew the trumpets regularly before the Ark of the covenant. This was not casual music. It was ordered, Spirit-filled, prophetic praise.

Notice that the text says they "ministered." Their audience was not the crowd, but Yehovah. Praise was ministry to Him first, and then ministry through Him to the people. When Jehoshaphat later sent singers out ahead of the army (2 Chronicles 20), it was this same priestly principle at work. Worship confounded the enemy and cleared the way for victory.

This reminds us to test our own worship today. Much of modern worship has shifted into the mold of a concert - lights, volume, and atmosphere focused more on the performer and the crowd than on Yehovah. When worship becomes self - gratification instead of ministry to Him, it loses its priestly power. True worship does not entertain the flesh but exalts the King. We must guard against turning worship into a show and return to ministering before His presence in Spirit and in truth.

Worship as Warfare

Throughout Scripture, worship is presented as a weapon. When Saul was tormented by an evil spirit, David's harp drove it away (1 Samuel 16:23). When Paul and Silas sang in prison, chains broke and doors opened (Acts 16:25-26). When Jehoshaphat's army faced overwhelming odds, the singers led the way, and God Himself set ambushes against their enemies (2 Chronicles 20:21-22).

The walls of Jericho also fell to a procession of worship. Priests carried the Ark and blew the trumpets, while the people shouted at God's command (Joshua 6:20). It was not military strength but worshipful obedience that brought down the walls.

In Revelation, heavenly worship shapes the future of the earth. Harps and bowls of incense represent the prayers and songs of the saints (Revelation 5:8). A great multitude sings a new song before the throne and before the Lamb. At the sound of worship, heaven responds, angels move, and the final victory of Messiah unfolds.

The Levites modeled that praise is not filler. It is warfare. It shifts the atmosphere, breaks oppression, and welcomes the manifest presence of God. In the Temple, music surrounded the Ark as a shield of praise. In Messiah, our worship becomes both incense before God and a sword against the enemy.

This is why we must never treat worship lightly. What you sing, how you play, and who you are ministering to make all the difference. Worship is not performance; it is priestly warfare.

And as we continue, Janice Baca will take us even deeper into the heart of worship by exploring the meaning of the **mizmor** - the psalm, the song that rises like incense to our King.

Teaching Takeaways

- David appointed thousands of Levites for musical ministry. Worship was central, not optional.

- Levites sang and played not for entertainment, but to minister to Yehovah Himself.

- Worship was constant, morning and evening, surrounding sacrifices, Feasts, and daily service.

- Elisha called for music to usher in the Spirit so the prophetic gift could flow.

- Paul and Silas sang in prison, and their worship released a supernatural intervention.

- Worship is warfare: at Jericho walls fell, in battle enemies were routed, and in Revelation heaven responds.

- Modern worship often resembles a concert. True priestly worship is not self - gratification but ministry before Yehovah.

- Worship is incense before God and a sword against the enemy.

Reflections for the Reader

- Do you view worship as a ministry to God or as an event for yourself?

- How often do you intentionally create an atmosphere of worship in your home, car, or personal life?

- In times of fear or oppression, do you use worship as a weapon, lifting your voice in praise until the heaviness breaks?

- Have you ever noticed how worship stirs up the gifts of the Spirit in you or others, as it did for Elisha?

- Do you believe that your worship can release supernatural interventions in your life or in the lives of others?

- Is your worship more focused on God's presence, or does it sometimes slip into performance and self-focus? What needs to shift?

- What do you think it means that heaven itself is filled with worship - and how does that reshape the way you sing here and now?

How to Walk This Out Practically

- **Make worship daily.** Sing psalms, hymns, and spiritual songs not just in gatherings but in your home, car, and private time.

- **Invite the Spirit.** Use music to set the atmosphere for prayer and prophetic flow, as Elisha did.

- **Worship in the midnight hour.** When faced with trials, choose to pray and sing instead of complain. Expect Yah to release supernatural intervention.

- **Guard focus.** Refuse to let worship become about performance. Keep your heart and attention fixed on ministering before His presence.

- **Use music for healing.** Play or sing songs of truth when you or others feel weary, anxious, or tormented.

- **Be a trumpet.** Let your worship declare truth boldly, silencing lies and shifting the spiritual atmosphere around you.

Prayer Activation

Father Yehovah, thank You for the gift of worship. Teach me to minister to You first, not to people. Let my songs and prayers rise as incense before Your throne.

Help me to see worship as warfare. Remind me to lift my voice in praise when I feel surrounded, to sing when I feel weak, and to trust that You are enthroned on the praises of Your people.

Let worship stir up the gifts of Your Spirit within me. As Elisha called for music to usher in Your presence, help me to lean on worship to draw near to You and hear Your voice clearly. Let my worship break chains like Paul and Silas experienced, releasing supernatural interventions in my life and in my community.

Father, forgive me for times I have made worship about myself rather than about You. Guard my heart from the trap of performance. Restore to me the joy of ministering before You in Spirit and truth.

Fill me with Your Spirit so that I may worship in truth. Let my life carry the sound of praise into my home, my community, and every place I go. May my worship open the gates for Your presence and close the door on the enemy.

Yeshua, I give You my song, my sound, and my heart. Be glorified in me. Amen.

As we have seen, worship was never meant to be entertainment. It is ministry to Yehovah, warfare in the Spirit, and the sound of heaven breaking into the earth. Yet what if worship carries even more than we have understood? What if, hidden within the very language of Scripture, there is a depth to worship that reveals a miraculous gift for the end days - a gift that not only exalts God but also drives out darkness, brings healing, and cuts down the enemy?

In the next chapter, my dear sister and fellow laborer in the Word, **Janice Baca**, takes us deeper into this mystery. Drawing on her study of the Hebrew root *zamar* and the word *mizmor* - the very word that gives us "psalm" - she reveals what she calls the gift of **God-singing**. Her research through ancient manuscripts uncovers a long-forgotten spiritual gift that David himself understood, a gift that may be vital for the battles we face in these last days.

It is my joy to hand this over to her voice now, as she unpacks for us the power of the *mizmor* and shows how true priestly worship is more than melody - it is a weapon, a healing balm, and a supernatural gift of the Spirit.

Chapter 9: The Mizmor - God-Singing

Gracious provided by Janice F. Baca

Spiritual Gift of Power of God-Singing

Let me invite you right into the heart of my journey - a journey that I hope will ignite something in you as well. I love to sing to Yehovah, not just because He is worthy, but because I've seen and felt the power that true worship unlocks. When I lift my voice and dance before Elohim (God), it's not as a performance - it's a real encounter. I feel His presence rush in, dissolving my fears and giving me victory over battles I never thought I could win. Here's the most exciting part: this isn't just my story. The same power of song and dance is available for you - especially in these extraordinary times. Worship is so much more than a ritual; it's an invitation for heaven to meet earth in the middle of our everyday struggles. I've experienced deliverance, healing, and breakthrough, and I believe you can too. Sometimes it's hard to describe just how much praise and worship can change a situation, but the Scriptures are filled with stories that show what's possible. Think about Paul and Silas, locked in prison - yet their singing and prayers flung the doors wide open. That's the kind of wonder I want you to discover as you read through my research. Let's step into this adventure together and see what miracles are waiting when we truly sing to Yehovah!

And at midnight Sha'ul and Silas were praying and singing songs to Elohim, and the prisoners were listening to them. And suddenly a great earthquake took place, so that the foundations of the prison

82

were shaken, **and immediately all the doors were opened and all the chains came loose**. Acts 16:25-26 ISR (emphasis mine)

Additionally, when I read stories like King Jehoshaphat's in Scripture. I can picture the fear and uncertainty that must have gripped Judah as enemies surrounded them. Instead of charging into battle, Jehoshaphat led his people to pray, fast, and - most powerfully - send singers out ahead to praise Elohim! Their worship wasn't just a ritual; it was their weapon. The songs they lifted up brought confusion to the enemy, turning the tide of the battle without anyone even lifting a sword. I imagine the overwhelming relief and joy as Judah gathered the spoils and returned home, knowing they had experienced Elohim's deliverance and peace in a way that could only come through trusting Him and praising with their whole hearts.

And after consulting with the people, he appointed **those who should sing to יהוה**, and **who should praise the splendour of set-apartness**, as they went out before the army and were saying, "Give thanks to יהוה, for His loving - commitment is everlasting." **And when they began singing and praising, יהוה set ambushes against the children of Ammon, Mo'aḇ, and Mount Sě'ir, who had come against Yehuḏah, and they were smitten**. 2 Chronicles 20:21-22 ISR (emphasis mine)

Furthermore, Psalm 146:6 - 9 instructs us that when we exalt Yehovah, it is a weapon like a two-edged sword that takes vengeance on our enemies.

Let the exaltation of Ěl be in their mouth, and a two - edged sword in their hand, to execute vengeance on the nations, punishments on the peoples; to bind their sovereigns with chains, and their nobles with iron bands; to execute on them the written right-ruling; a splendour it is for all His lovingly-committed ones. Praise Yah! Psalm 146:6-9

But before we go any further, I want you to pause for a moment and imagine this: the New Testament lists out an incredible array of spiritual gifts - administration, apostleship, discernment, evangelism, exhortation, faith, giving, healing, helps, hospitality, knowledge, leadership, mercy, prophecy, serving, speaking in tongues, teaching, wisdom - and then, tucked right alongside those, is something absolutely electrifying: power of God-singing.[1] Did that surprise you? It surprised me! This isn't just any singing - this is a gift so powerful it was known by King David and the first disciples, but it's been hidden from most of us until now. Can you picture yourself discovering a gift that actually brings the miracles of heaven into the room? When I uncovered this through deep research and ancient Cochin Hebrew New Testament manuscripts, it felt like finding a treasure meant for this exact moment in history - these very days when the world needs Elohim's power more than ever.[2] Just imagine: when you step into power of God-singing, you're not just making music - you're releasing a force that can drive out darkness, heal the sick, bring you clarity, and fill your space with God's strength and might. What could happen if you dared to try?

Digging in the Hebrew Aramaic Lexicons and Dictionaries

Let's take a journey together into the heart of the Hebrew Bible. Have you ever wondered what a word really meant in its original setting? I know I have! When I dig into the Hebrew or Aramaic words in the Tanakh (Old Testament), I often reach for all the best

84

dictionaries and lexicons, hoping to uncover the true meaning behind each word. But honestly, it isn't always straightforward - sometimes, it feels like detective work! Imagine if you and I could travel back in time and ask the original authors what they intended. Since we can't, we have to piece it together as best we can. That's why I'm excited to explore the ancient Hebrew root זמר (zayin - mem - resh) with you. Who knows? Maybe what we discover will spark something new - and even help you tap into a bit of "God-power" in your own God-song!

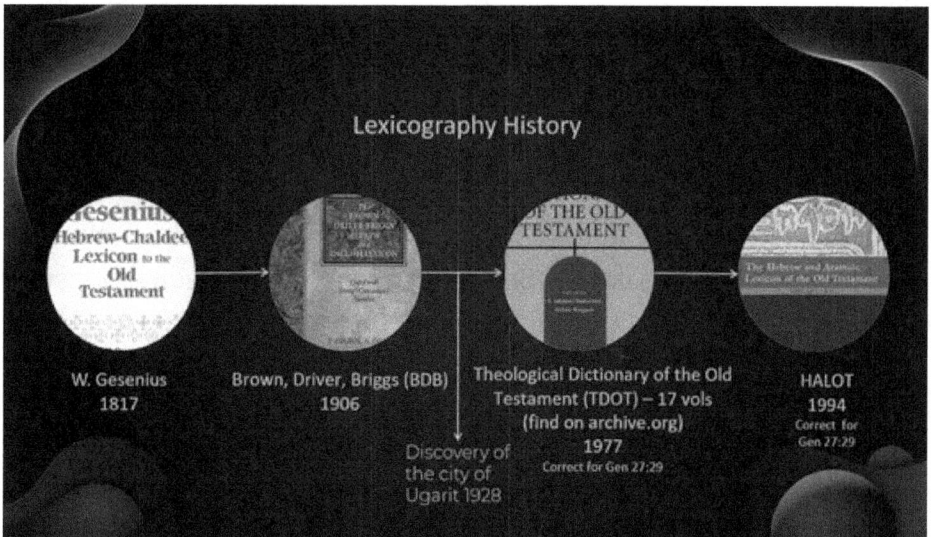

Lexicography History

W. Gesenius 1817	Brown, Driver, Briggs (BDB) 1906	Theological Dictionary of the Old Testament (TDOT) – 17 vols (find on archive.org) 1977 Correct for Gen 27:29	HALOT 1994 Correct for Gen 27:29
		Discovery of the city of Ugarit 1928	

Let's roll up our sleeves and dive into a bit of word detective work together! Have you ever wondered what a single Hebrew word might really mean, or how many layers it could have? I love digging into this kind of mystery, and I want to bring you along for the ride. When I explore the root זמר (zayin - mem - resh), I find myself flipping through pages of brilliant resources like *Gesenius' Hebrew and Chaldee Lexicon to the Old Testament Scriptures*,[3] *Brown Driver Briggs Hebrew and English Lexicon* (BDB),[4] *The*

Theological Dictionary of the Old Testament (TDOT),[5] and the *Hebrew, Aramaic Lexicon of the Old Testament* (HALOT).[6] Here's what's fascinating: this one root זמר (zayin - mem - resh), can mean (1) to sing (with or without instruments) and dance, (2) strength or might, and (3) the act of plucking strings, pruning, or cutting down. Isn't it amazing how much richness is packed into a single word? Of course, the search isn't easy - sometimes I wish you and I could hop in a time machine and ask the original writers ourselves! Since we can't, we have to become history detectives, piecing together clues from old dictionaries, ancient manuscripts, and context. It's not an exact science, but that's what makes it so exciting. So, as we go through these discoveries, I hope you'll feel inspired to see how much adventure and meaning can hide in just one ancient word.

To begin, let's step into the fascinating story of Hebrew grammar and linguistics! Instead of a dry review, imagine yourself alongside ancient scribes and storytellers. Did you know that what we call "Hebrew" was once known as the "tongue of Canaan"? In fact, Hebrew and Aramaic began as one language before branching off. The name "Hebrew" itself didn't appear until much later - so much so that even the historian Josephus, writing in the First Century, didn't really distinguish between Hebrew and Aramaic. During King Hezekiah's time, his men referred to their language as "Yudahite" when speaking to the Assyrian invaders (2 Kings 18:26). And in the Assyrian records of that era, the land was called "Yudaea" (Judaea), while the Scriptures describe it as the "tongue of Canaan" (Isaiah 19:18). Even ancient Egypt was sometimes called Canaan![7] Isn't it amazing how language connects us to the past?

Now, let's meet an interesting figure in the research of Hebrew study - Heinrich Friedrich Wilhelm Gesenius (1786-1842). Imagine us sitting together, flipping through old books and marveling at the work of a true language detective! The editors of the BDB lexicon even call Gesenius the father of modern Hebrew lexicography. He published his groundbreaking work on Hebrew grammar back in 1817 before turning his attention to the world of dictionaries. Later, the Brown-Driver-Briggs lexicon (maybe you've heard of it?) was published in 1906 and built on Gesenius' earlier work, thanks to editors Francis Brown, Samuel Rolles Driver, and Charles Augustus Briggs. That's why it's called Brown-Driver-Briggs, or BDB for short. It's like a treasure chest of discoveries, but remember, it's only the first stage in our adventure of understanding the language of the Hebrew Bible.

Discovery of the City of Ugarit

Let me take you on a little adventure - a real archaeological treasure hunt! Picture this: it's 1928, a farmer, just doing his daily work, stumbles across an ancient tomb in his field. That single moment sparks a wave of excitement, drawing archaeologists from all over to explore what turns out to be the ancient city of Ugarit, nestled on the northern coast of Syria. Can you imagine the thrill as hundreds of tablets are uncovered from the palace and temple ruins? Over 1,500 of these tablets have been published, each one opening a window into a world that peaked between the fifteenth and thirteenth centuries BCE - a time when Ugarit was buzzing with stories and songs.

Let's step into the shoes of an explorer together! Imagine the excitement as archaeologists and locals in Ugarit sifted through the earth and uncovered clay tablets inscribed with a mysterious script (called cuneiform script) - a language the world had never

87

seen before. This language, later called Ugaritic, named after the city, turned out to be a key that unlocked new secrets about the Hebrew language. Isn't it amazing how ancient discoveries can shine fresh light on something we thought we already understood?

Here's where it gets really personal for us as lovers of language: Ugaritic and Hebrew share many similarities, so these discoveries gave us new ways to understand Hebrew grammar and vocabulary. Let me share one of my favorite linguistic puzzles with you. In Genesis 27:29, there's a word - יִשְׁתַּחֲוּוּ (yish'chavu'u), meaning "to bow down" - that has a rare verb structure called the Hishtafel. For years, the respected Brown Driver Briggs (BDB) lexicon guessed at its origin root, thinking the root was שחה (shin – chet – hey) based on clever letter swapping (called metathesis). But then, thanks to the Ugaritic tablets, scholars discovered this exact verb form and realized the true root was חוי (chet – vav – yod) - a discovery that flipped the old understanding on its head!

This is such a powerful reminder for you and me: even the most celebrated dictionaries are only steppingstones on the journey of discovery. Our understanding keeps growing with every new clue. That's why, when I learned about the misstep in BDB and saw how later resources like TDOT and HALOT corrected it, I felt inspired to question everything I thought I knew about the root זמר (zayin - mem - resh) root. What hidden depths might we find if we keep exploring together?

Why does this matter for us? Because it reminds us that even the most respected dictionaries and lexicons are really just best guesses - snapshots in an ongoing journey of discovery. This revelation made me rethink everything I thought I knew about the root זמר (zayin - mem - resh). What if, thanks to the spirit of adventure and a willingness to dig deeper, we could uncover an even richer meaning together? Are you ready to see where this exploration takes us?

The Piel Stem System: Intensifier!

Let's dive into something truly fascinating together! I've noticed (and scholars have noticed) that every single verb formed from the root זמר (zayin - mem - resh) in the Hebrew Bible appears in the Piel banyan stem. Why should you care about the Piel stem? Because it's not just any verb form - it's an intensifier! It packs extra energy, intent, and sometimes even a sense of causing something to happen. And here's something fun: even top scholars like Joüon-Muraoka (whose grammar book is still the go - to for Biblical Hebrew) admit that the Piel is mysterious - "the most elusive of the Hebrew conjugations."[8]

So, what does this mean for us as we explore God-singing? It means there's a deeper layer to discover! Let's make it real with an example. Take the Hebrew root שבר (shin – vet – resh). In the basic Qal stem, שָׁבַר (shavar) means, "He broke." No big deal, right? But switch it to the Piel, שִׁבֵּר (shiber), and suddenly it's, "He shattered!" or "He smashed!" - full of passion and intent. Can you picture the difference? He didn't just break it; he meant to, and he did it with all his might!

That's the kind of intensity we're talking about when we see זמר (zayin - mem - resh) in the Piel stem in the Bible. This isn't casual, background singing. This is powerful, purposeful, God-driven singing - done with heart, intention, and maybe even a little bit of holy fire!

Let's keep digging into the Piel stem together! I love how Scholar and Pastor Timothy Smith, in his paper "Review of The Piel Stem System," really brings the text to life by showing us just how many ways the Piel verb stem can be used. Out of the thirty-three uses he lists, I've picked out a few that I think you'll find especially interesting as we explore the root זמר (zayin - mem - resh).

The 1926 Hebrew Grammar by C.T. Wood and H.C.O. Lanchester (both of Cambridge) briefly states that "the pixel usually expresses vigor or eagerness of action" (p. 72) but later adds that "the piel is frequently causative, especially in stative verbs; e.g., 'he caused to learn,' i.e., taught." (p. 73).

Three of the 33 uses quoted are:

20. Multiple subjects in the same act

21. Multiple objects of the same act

22. Multiple occurrences of the same act. [9]

After searching through ten Hebrew Grammars, Rosenthal's Aramaic Grammar, and even a Syriac Grammar for comparison, I've gathered a treasure trove of examples. I can't wait to share some of these discoveries with you as we dive into how the Piel brings powerful meaning to God-singing!

What truly excites me is discovering how the Tanakh habitually uses the Piel verb stem for זמר (zayin - mem - resh) with such intention and divine purpose. It feels as if the language itself is reaching out, urging us to see that this word isn't just about singing, strength, or even plucking strings - it's all of those, supercharged with passion and meaning! I can't help but smile at how the Piel verb stem cranks up each meaning, making the experience of God

90

- singing feel so alive and deliberate. It's like the text invites us to join in … singing with all our heart and purpose.

So, when I dig into these words, I'm not just looking at their history - I'm searching for the deeper story the context and verb stem reveal. And honestly, my curiosity only grew after conversations with my Biblical Hebrew professor (who's also a Cohen in Jerusalem!) and after exploring the Cochin Hebrew New Testament manuscripts (Cambridge MS Oo.1.32, Oo.1.16.1, Oo.1.16.2). Their insights made me stop and wonder: What powerful message might be waiting for us when we look at the root זמר (zayin - mem - resh) through this lens of intensity and purpose? Let's unpack this together!

Power of God-Singing Described by a Cohen?

Let me take you into a moment that sparked my curiosity and changed the way I see the word זִמְרָת (zimrat). Picture me sitting in my Biblical Hebrew Course at the Israel Institute of Biblical Studies, listening intently as my Cohen instructor shared something that made my eyes light up. He explained that זִמְרָת - the ancient, Piel form of the word זמר (zayin - mem - resh) - might mean so much more than just "singing." What if it's actually "Power of God singing," or as he called it, "God-singing"? Imagine: music so filled with divine strength that it's not just a song, but a force!

If that's true, then all those old etymological roots - (1) Song, (2) Might, and even (3) Pruning or Cutting down - aren't just definitions, but are woven together into something alive and powerful. I got even more excited when I came across Chaim Bentorah's word study, which suggests זמר (zayin - mem - resh) could mean a song that literally cut down your enemies! Suddenly, these ideas weren't just theories - they felt like an invitation to discover something miraculous.

That's why I've been digging through the Tanakh and the Cochin Hebrew New Testament manuscripts with new eyes and a fresh sense of wonder. What if this unique, miracle - filled singing is especially important for the end of days, when the one hundred forty-four thousand will sing a mysterious song that only they can learn? I'd love for you to imagine this with me: What would it mean for you to step into the power of God-singing in your own life?

God-Singing in the Tanakh (Old Testament)

In Exodus 15:2, written in Ancient Hebrew, we find the archaic form of the root זמר (zayin - mem - resh) as זִמְרָת (zimrat, H2176)[10] in the Song of the Sea (Exodus 15:2). Thus, if we apply the theories that the etymological root זמר (zayin - mem - resh) means God-singing with music and dance, or cutting down our enemies in the song, then the Song of the Sea is a song of victory and may even be a war song that exhibits great power when sung! Additionally, the Song of the Sea is the first and oldest song in the Tanakh, and it is my theory that it may also be the final song sung at the end of days because Yehovah is the first and the last[11] and His song is first and will also be His last. And the first song may also be the final song sung through the one hundred forty-four thousand in Revelation 14. To further complicate matters, there appear to be missing verses discovered of the Song of the Sea in Exodus 15 within the Dead Sea Scrolls (DSS),[12] and this could be the reason why others cannot learn the song, for these could be the verses that has been long lost from the ancient of days. For if this is indeed the song of the one hundred and forty-four thousand, then the words, tune, and frequency must be imparted to the one hundred forty-four thousand miraculously at the end of days. Therefore, it is for these reasons, and many others, that I believe the song of the one hundred forty-four thousand will be the renewed Song of the Sea because it is the final song to be sung in the latter days!

King David, The God-Singer

Let me bring you into one of my favorite stories - King David truly grasped the life-changing power of praise and worship. For him, singing wasn't just about melodies; it was spiritual warfare, something I like to call God-singing. Picture young David, harp in hand, called to King Saul's side because Saul was plagued by tormenting spirits sent to him by Yehovah for his disobedience. I always imagine the tension in that room. The air must have felt heavy until David began to play. His music didn't just entertain - it brought real peace and relief, driving away those dark spirits, just as 1 Samuel 16:23 describes. That's the kind of miraculous impact God-singing can have!

And the Spirit of יהוה turned aside from Sha'ul, and an evil spirit from יהוה troubled him. and the servants of Sha'ul said to him, "Look, now, an evil spirit from Elohim is troubling you. Please, let our master command your servants who are before you, to seek out a man who is a skilled player on the lyre. And it shall be that when the evil spirit from Elohim is upon you, that he shall play with his hand, and you be well. And Sha'ul said to his servants, "Please get me a man that plays well, and bring him to me." And one of the servants answered and said, "Look, I have seen a son of Yishai the Běyth Leḥemite, **who knows how to play, a brave one, and a**

man of battle, and skilled in words, and a handsome man. And יהוה is with him." 1 Samuel 16:14-18 ISR (emphasis mine)

And it came to be, whenever the *evil* spirit from Elohim was upon Sha'ul, that Dawiḏ would take a lyre and play it with his hand. **Then Sha'ul would become refreshed and well, and the evil spirit would leave him**. 1 Samuel 16:23 ISR (emphasis mine)

I love how 2 Samuel 23:1 calls King David the "sweet God-singer of Israel" (זְמִ רֹות zimrat, from the root זמר (zayin - mem - resh)). That phrase jumps off the page for me because it recognizes David's one-of-a-kind, miraculous spiritual gift. It's like Scripture is inviting us to see David not just as a king or warrior, but as someone who sang so powerfully to Elohim that it became part of his identity - and maybe, if we let it, become part of ours too.

And these are the last words of Dawiḏ, the saying of Dawiḏ son of Yishai, the saying of the man raised above, the anointed of the Elohim of Ya'aqob, and the sweet **God-singer** (זְמִ רֹות zimrat) **of Yisra'ĕl**: 2 Samuel 23:1 ISR (emphasis [and addition] mine)

I can't help but feel inspired when I think about King David recognizing his miraculous gift from Yehovah. Imagine him pouring his heart into the Psalms - those mizmorim - which I truly believe are God-songs written as a legacy for all future generations of God-singers like you and me. It's a little sad to realize that many English translations leave out the special introductions to these mizmorim. Those opening lines often call out to the chief Musician, inviting everyone to get ready for a power of God-song, like in Psalm 20:1. Can you picture the anticipation building before the music even begins?

To the chief Musician, A **Psalm** (מזמור mizmor) of David. Psalms 20:1[13] ISR (emphasis [and addition] mine)

Let me invite you to imagine King David not just as a king or a poet, but as a master strategist whose weapon was worship! I love picturing him, the sweet God - singer, fully convinced that singing to Yehovah could cut down his enemies and turn the tide of battle. I'm struck by how he didn't just keep this gift to himself - he organized whole teams of singers and musicians, setting them in place as a kind of spiritual army. Can you picture the energy and faith it took to send singers ahead as part of a military campaign, like in 1 Chronicles 25:1? Or to call everyone together to lift up praises before Elohim, as in 1 Chronicles 15:16 and 24?

What amazes me even more is that David involved his military commanders, instructing them to help appoint families of worshipers - people like Asaph, Heman, and Jeduthun - to sing and prophesy as an actual military duty, a God-given assignment. That's how much David believed in the miraculous power of God-singing. I wonder what would happen if we approached worship with the same passion and expectancy - that when we sing, Yehovah's power fills the place and changes everything!

And Dawiḏ spoke to the leaders of the Lěwites to appoint their brothers the singers with instruments of song, harps, and lyres, and cymbals, to lift up the voice with joy. 1 Chronicles 15:16 ISR

And Dawiḏ and the commanders of the army separated for the service some of the sons of Asaph, and of Hěman, and of Yeḏuthun, **who should prophesy with lyres, with harps, and with cymbals**, 1 Chronicles 25:1a ISR (emphasis mine)

95

What really excites me is how several Psalms actually invite us - yes, you and me - to step into God-singing ourselves. When I read verses like Psalm 81:2, Psalm 98:5, Psalm 147:1, and Psalm 149:3, I feel as though Scripture is calling us to join a chorus of worshipers across generations, lifting our voices with passion and purpose. Can you imagine the joy of adding your own God-song to that ancient, powerful melody?

Lift up a **God-song** (ז.מ.ר.ה - zimra) and beat the tambourine, the pleasant lyre, and with the harp." Psalms 81:2 ISR (emphasis [and Hebrew addition] mine)

God-Sing (ז.מ.רו - zamru) to Yehovah with the lyre, with the lyre and the voice of a God song (ז.מ.ר.ה - zimra)," Psalms 98:5 ISR (emphasis [and addition] mine)

"Praise Yah! For it is good to **God-sing** (ז.מ.ר.ה - zamra) praises to our Elohim. For it is pleasant – praise is fitting." Psalms 147:1 ISR (emphasis [and addition] mine)

"Let them praise His Name in a dance; Let them **God-sing** (י.ז.מ.רו - yezamru) praises to Him with the tambourine and lyre." Psalms 149:3 ISR (emphasis [and addition] mine)

I find it so inspiring that King David set an example not just for his own time but for us, too - especially for those of us living in these challenging and dark days. He didn't see God-singing as something optional or merely uplifting; he saw it as a vital spiritual weapon! When David played and sang before King Saul, the darkness had to retreat - demons literally fled. That wasn't just a story for the past; I truly believe this is meant for us now. Imagine what could happen if we approached God-singing with the same faith and expectation. When we lift our voices to Yehovah, we can

96

believe for victory, deliverance, and healing to break through in our own lives and in the world around us.

The Chief Prevailer!

Let me invite you into the story behind King David - a power of God-singer, a warrior, and a musician whose songs have inspired generation after generation. When I think about the מזמורים mizmorim (plural form of the mizmor, Power of God-song) of the Psalms, I see so much more than ancient poetry. David's music was a declaration of victory! He used unique language, not just to celebrate, but to paint the music leader - the chief musician - as a true prevailer (root: נצח - nun - tsade - chet). Imagine that: the person leading the worship wasn't just keeping everyone in tune, but was leading the people into victory through the power of song! Wait… What? Is the Chief Musician more than a leader of music?

Here's something I want to share from my own journey of study: I used to overlook the value of older lexicons and dictionaries, but I've learned that every resource has something to offer. Take BDB, for example - it references Jerome, an early theologian who suggested that "choirmaster," (root נצח (nun – tsade – chet)), could be better understood as "the overcomer," "victorious," or "prevailer." That gives the phrase "to the chief Musician…" in Psalm 20:1 a whole new depth of understanding. It's not just about music; it's about overcoming, about victory! And when I read that Eusebius and Theodocia thought this idea might be especially important for the end of days,[14] I couldn't help but agree. What if Yehovah is inviting us, right now, to become prevailers through the power of God-music?

97

To the chief Musician, A **Psalm** (מזמור mizmor) of David. Psalms 20:1 ISR (emphasis [and addition] mine)

Additionally, I love how the story of the prophet Habakkuk, writing around 612 BCE just before the Babylonian invasion, feels so relatable - he moves from wrestling with questions and doubts to boldly expressing faith in Yehovah's power and deliverance. What really stands out to me is how Habakkuk 3 uses the root נצח (nun - tsade - chet), the same word for "prevailer," in verse 19. The final line could even be translated as, "For the prevailer (לַמְ‏נַ‏צֵּ‏ח‏ בִּ‏נְ‏גִ‏ינוֹתָ‏י) on my stringed instruments!" I can just picture Habakkuk leading with his song, prevailing through music - an encouragement for you and me that our own songs of faith can shift the atmosphere and lead to victory, even in the toughest moments.

If מְ‏נַ‏צֵּ‏ח (menatzeach, root: נצח (nun - tsade - chet)), is describing a leader who is not only a leader of music, but also describes an overcomer *with or through* music, then the leading overcomer will guide the people to ultimate victory at the end of days - including overcoming the dragon and the beast described in Revelation 12 and 13, including overcoming the demonic! And I believe that Psalm 91 is key to victory and should be prayed, proclaimed, and even sung every day![15]

As I wrap up this journey with you, I want to share just how much I've come to appreciate the treasure hunt of exploring lexicons, dictionaries, and every detail of Biblical Hebrew. Each word feels like a clue in an unfolding mystery! If Jerome is right about the root נצח (nun, tsade, chet) pointing to a "lead prevailer," and if Eusebius and Theodocia are onto something, then maybe you and I are being invited to rediscover a powerful, overlooked spiritual gift for our own time. What if the power of God-music is meant for us - right now, in these days? I hope this inspires you to dig deeper, ask bold questions, and seek out the spiritual gifts that can bring victory and hope in your own life!

Miracle Singers in the Hebrew New Testament!

Imagine holding in your hands a piece of history: the Cochin Hebrew New Testament (Cambridge MS Oo.1.32, Oo.1.16.1, Oo.1.16.2), discovered in Cochin, India, by Claudius Buchanan in 1803 in the synagogue of the Malabari Black Jews. While the manuscript may be imperfect, it is nothing short of remarkable - a treasure that has captivated scholars and readers around the world. What makes it so fascinating is its unique blend of late Second Temple Hebrew grammar with Mishnaic Hebrew and Aramaic influences, setting it apart from any other known Hebrew New Testament manuscripts. Even more intriguing are its Tanakh (Old Testament) references, especially the distinct use of the word זמר (zayin - mem - resh). As you explore the manuscript's verses, you'll notice the deliberate choice to highlight a very specific kind of singing. The authors wanted their readers - not just to read, but to feel and understand - the subtle differences between each type of song. If we follow their lead and apply the same verb stem found in the Tanakh, we can see that every instance of the word זמר (zayin - mem - resh) in the Cochin Hebrew New Testament appears in the Piel verb stem, hinting at a singing that is both intentional and full of passion.

But before we dive deeper, take a moment to notice how the Cochin Hebrew New Testament thoughtfully distinguishes between singing and praising in its translations of Cochin Hebrew Matthew

11:17 and Acts 16:25. In Cochin Hebrew Matthew 11:17, the phrase is simple and direct: "We sing" (שיר - shir). In contrast, Cochin Hebrew Acts 16:25 describes Paul and Silas as praying and "praising." The choice of words here isn't arbitrary - it invites you to picture the scene vividly, to sense the difference between casual singing and heartfelt praise. This distinction isn't about singing to God with intensity or intention; it's about painting a nuanced, living image of these moments for every reader.

and they say, 'We **sing** (שירים - shirim) for you and you are not dancing. And we **lament** (קונים - konnim) for you, but you do not weep." (Cochin Matthew 11:17 (emphasis [and Hebrew addition] mine))

And in the middle of the night, Paul and Silas were praying and **praising** (משבחים - meshabchim) Elodim (God), and prisoners were listening to them. Cochin Acts 16:25 (emphasis [and addition] mine)

Now, picture yourself among the first readers of the Cochin Hebrew New Testament, encountering verses that celebrate the spiritual gift of the God-song. These passages don't just tell; they urge the community to find strength in the power of a God-song and to truly prove themselves through God - singing. You can feel the difference - this isn't the everyday singing mentioned in Cochin Hebrew Matthew 11:17 or Acts 16:25. Instead, as you read Colossians 3:16 in this manuscript, you're invited into a type of singing that, through the Piel verb stem, bursts forth with intention and intensity. It's as if the manuscript is calling you to join in, to sing with passion and purpose.

And speak to your soul in a **God-song** (מזמור - mizmor) and praise. And sing God songs (מזמרים - mizmorim) being in the Spirit."

100

Cochin Hebrew Ephesians 5:19 (emphasis [and Hebrew addition] mine)

And let the word of the Messiah dwell in your sons in all wisdom, and learn proving yourselves with singings (שירות - shirot) and praises (תושבחות - teshveachot), and (intensely and intentionally) **God-singing** (מזמרים - mezamrim) to the Lord in your hearts." Cochin Hebrew Colossians 3:16 (emphasis [and Hebrew addition] mine)

Next, imagine the scene in Cochin Hebrew Luke 15:25: the prodigal son returns home, and the air is alive with more than just praise - there's an eruption of God-Singing, a joyful celebration that fills every corner of the house. You can almost hear the music and feel the embrace of a family reunited. In these moments, the singing becomes more than intense; it transforms into a Piel causative singing, a sound that embodies the deep love Yehovah holds between parents and their children. Through this God-singing, we're invited to glimpse how Yehovah Himself rejoices and loves when His lost children find their way back to Him.

And the eldest son was in the city. And then he came towards the house, and he heard great sound (intense and intentional) **God-singing** (זמר - zemer). Cochin Hebrew Luke 15:25 (emphasis [and Hebrew addition] mine)

Now, imagine hearing the words of Cochin Hebrew Romans 15:9 as if they're spoken directly to you: even when we find ourselves scattered among the nations, we're called to lift our voices and God-sing to the name of Yehovah. No matter where we are, this invitation remains - a personal call to join in a song that unites us across every distance.

And the nations will praise Yehovah for the substitution of mercy upon them as it is written, 'I will give thanks to You in the nations, and I will (intensely and intentionally, continually) **God-sing** (אזמר - azamer) to Your name!'" Cochin Hebrew Romans 15:9 (emphasis [and Hebrew addition] mine)

Let's pause and listen closely to Cochin Hebrew 1 Corinthians 14:15. Here, Paul isn't just instructing - he's inviting each of us to discover and use our miraculous spiritual gifts with real understanding, especially the gift of God-singing. Imagine being told that when you sing to God, you're tapping into something truly miraculous - a unique gift from Elohim Himself. This isn't just music; it's an act of worship infused with power and might. So the next time you lift your voice in song, remember: you're participating in something extraordinary, a spiritual gift that connects you directly to the divine.

What now I do is pray in the spirit and pray in understanding. And what I God-sing (מזמר - mezamer) in the Spirit, I will (intensely and intentionally, continually) **God-sing** (אזמר - azamer) with understanding.'" Cochin Hebrew 1 Corinthians 14:15 (emphasis [and Hebrew addition] mine)

Now, imagine gathering with others and letting the miracle gift of God-singing flow through you, just as Cochin Hebrew 1 Corinthians 14:26 encourages. Your voice, joined with others, becomes a source of strength and encouragement - a living expression of faith that uplifts everyone present.

I say now, my brothers, that truly as you gather together, those of you who have a **God-song** (מזמור -mizmor), or an utterance; or if there is a word of knowledge, or an interpretation: let all this be to build them." Cochin Hebrew 1 Corinthians 14:26 (emphasis [and Hebrew addition] mine)

Picture your faith as gold, tested and refined by fire. That's the powerful image 1 Peter paints in Cochin Hebrew 1 Peter 1:7 - our most challenging moments, our trials, can be transformed into a God-song. In the midst of refining, you're invited to find hope and beauty, letting your own God-song rise from the very heart of perseverance.

So that we may find your faith more honest than silver refined by fire, to (intensely, intentionally, continually) **God-sing** (זמר - zamer) and praise; and to praise when the day Yeshua Messiah is discovered." Cochin Hebrew 1 Peter 1:7 (emphasis [and Hebrew addition] mine)

Now, imagine the wisdom found in Cochin Hebrew James: when your heart is full of goodness and joy, God-singing isn't just encouraged - it's essential. The text uses the word (צריך - tzarich), meaning "need, should, must; necessary, required." It's as if the manuscript is gently reminding you that if your heart overflows with kindness, positivity, or gratitude, then singing to Elohim is not just an option, but a beautiful necessity. Your joyful heart naturally finds its voice in a song to the Divine.

And if one of you suffers anything, he must (צריך - tzarich) pray. And if one among you is of good heart, he must (צריך - tzarich) (intentionally and intensely, continually) **God-sing** (לזמר – lezamer) psalms." Cochin Hebrew James 5:13 (emphasis [and Hebrew addition] mine)

The End of Day God-Singers

Imagine yourself stepping into the world of *The Scroll of Mysteries: Cochin Hebrew Revelation*. [16] Here, you stand among three extraordinary groups of God-singers in the latter days: the twenty-four elders, the one hundred forty-four thousand, and those courageous souls who overcome the dragon and the beast - could you be counted among them? In these times of trials, battles, and troubles, the music is anything but ordinary. The text hints that these verses are filled with the זמר (zayin - mem - resh) Piel verb stem, painting a vivid picture of singing that is intentional, intense, and sometimes even unstoppable. It's a call not just to sing, but to pour your heart into every note - perhaps even to find yourself singing continually, carried by the passion of faith.

And they (intensely and intentionally, continually) **God-sang** (זמרו - zimru) a renewed song and said, "You are worthy to take the scroll and open its seals, for You were slain, and You redeemed us by Your own blood." Cochin Hebrew Revelation 5:9 (emphasis [and Hebrew addition] mine)

They were (intensely and intentionally) **God-singing** (מזמרים - mezamrim) the renewed song before the throne, the four living creatures, and the elders. No one was able to learn this song but the hundred and forty-four thousand that He redeemed from the ground." Cochin Hebrew Revelation 14:3 (emphasis [and Hebrew addition] mine)

They (intensely, and intentionally, continually) **God-sang** (מזמרים - mezamrim) the song of Moses and the song of the Lamb, saying, 'Great are the works of Yehovah, Elohim of Armies! Justice and truth are your ways, King of kings!' Cochin Hebrew Revelation 15:3 (emphasis [and Hebrew addition] mine)

Imagine facing the end of days - not just as a distant prophecy, but as a real, looming challenge that will test every ounce of your faith and courage. In these extraordinary times, survival alone isn't enough; we're called to overcome with the miraculous gifts Elohim provides. Picture Yehovah's people, you included, relying on the miracle gifts of the Holy Spirit - not just to endure, but to become a beacon for others in the darkest moments. This is why miraculous God - singing isn't just a spiritual extra; it's an essential weapon in the final battle. Through this gift, we find strength for healing, deliverance, clarity of mind, and even victories that go far beyond the battlefield. When the days grow severe, let your God-song rise - it just might be the miracle you and those around you need most.

Other Hebrew New Testament Manuscripts

As we come to the end of this study, I invite you to marvel with me at the uniqueness of the Cochin Hebrew New Testament manuscripts (Cambridge MS Oo.1.32, Oo.1.16.1, Oo.1.16.2). My curiosity led me to dive deep into a comparative analysis with other Hebrew New Testament manuscripts, zeroing in on the powerful word root זמר (zayin - mem - resh) across several key verses: Luke 15:25, Romans 15:9, Ephesians 5:19, Colossians 3:16, 1 Corinthians 14:15, 26, 1 Peter 1:7, James 5:13, and Revelation 5:9, 14:3, 15:3. What follows is not just a list, but the story of what makes this manuscript so extraordinary - a glimpse into the spiritual and linguistic treasures.

Paris 131[17] (Bibliothèque Sainte - Geneviève, MS. 131)

Luke 15:25: Yes, זמר (zayin - mem - resh) does appear, but it is used as a noun and not as a verb.

Romans 15:9: Yes, זמר (zayin - mem - resh) does appear as a verb.

1 Corinthians 14:15: Yes, זמר (zayin - mem - resh) does appear, but used in a different verb stem.

1 Corinthians 14:26: Yes, זמר (zayin - mem - resh) does appear as a verb.

Ephesians 5:19: Yes, זמר (zayin - mem - resh) does appear, but only used once as a verb and not as a noun.

Colossians 3:16: No, this word does not appear in this text.

James 5:13: Yes, זמר (zayin - mem - resh) does appear, but uses a different verb form than the Cochin Hebrew James.

Special Note: The Paris 131 is a Hebrew New Testament manuscript gifted to Pope Clement VIII and is a translation from Greek to Hebrew with some modifications.

The Hebrew Gospels of Catalonia Vat. ebr. 100[18] (Matthew, Mark, Luke, and John)

Luke 15:25: No, זמר (zayin - mem - resh) does not appear in this text.

Special Note: The Hebrew Gospels of Catalonia contain only Matthew, Mark, Luke, and John and are translations from the Catalan language into Hebrew.[19]

The Freiburg HS - 314[20] New Testament

No, זמר (zayin - mem - resh) does not appear on all accounts.

Special Note: The Freiburg HS - 314 is a nearly word - for - word translation from Greek to Hebrew.

The Manchester Gaster 1616[21] New Testament

Yes, זמר (zayin - mem - resh) does appear in all accounts, because it is a copy of the Cochin Hebrew New Testament.

Special Note: The Manchester Gaster 1616 is a corrupted copy of the Cochin Hebrew New Testament (Cambridge MS Oo.1.32, Oo.1.16.1, and Oo.1.16.2). The scribe included many marginal notes and made random changes, including removing most of the written names of Yehovah.

The Marseille MS 24[22] New Testament

Luke 15:24: No, זמר (zayin - mem - resh) does not appear.

Special Note: This manuscript contains Luke and Acts only.

The Shepreve [23]New Testament

James 5:13: Yes, זמר (zayin - mem - resh) does appear, but uses a different verb structure form from the Cochin Hebrew James.

Special Note: This manuscript is part of the collection of the British Royal Museum in *London, Roy MS 16 A II*. This manuscript was donated to the Museum by King George II as part of a group of manuscripts referred to as the 'Old Royal Library.' This handwritten manuscript was presented to King Henry VIII by John Shepreve, a noted Hebrew scholar at Corpus Christi College, Oxford University.[24]

Final Thoughts

Many of us knew in our hearts that singing praises to our Elohim would bring about victory and the destruction of our enemies, but our theory lacked academic evidence. However, this study *Power of God-Singing: In The Hebrew New Testament* conclusion gives great confidence to worshipers everywhere.

Oh, it is so amazing! The results of this comparative analysis are nothing short of electrifying: the Cochin Hebrew New Testament (Cambridge MS Oo.1.32, Oo.1.16.1, Oo.1.16.2) is in a league of its own! No other Hebrew New Testament manuscript on earth contains all the powerful Hebrew markers of the unique זמר (zayin - mem - resh) - the intense and intentional power of God-singing, expressed with the thrilling Piel verb stem. Imagine uncovering a manuscript that connects you directly to the epic worship of King David himself! These ancient words invite you to experience worship as a force so dynamic, so purposeful, that it echoes through the ages. This is your invitation: reflect on the extraordinary teachings of the Cochin Hebrew New Testament and boldly ask Yehovah for the gift of God-singing. When you step into this power, you're not just singing - you're driving away darkness, unlocking healing, and clearing your mind with every note. Don't wait - embrace this day, lift your voice, and God - sing to Yehovah with all your heart!

- Janice F Baca

Teaching Takeaways

- *Mizmor* (psalm) comes from *zamar* (to sing, play, cut down), showing worship as both praise and warfare.

- God Himself sings over His people (Zephaniah 3:17).

- Messiah joins the assembly in song (Hebrews 2:12), revealing divine participation in worship.

- Worship is not only expression but participation in God's own activity, releasing healing, deliverance, and victory.

- Singing is both intimacy with God and a weapon against His enemies.

Reflections for the Reader

- How does it change your worship to realize that God Himself sings over you?

- Do you see your songs as both praise and warfare? How might this reshape your daily worship?

- What situations in your life right now need the cutting, pruning power of *zamar* worship?

- Have you ever considered that when you worship, you are joining Messiah's own song in the assembly?

How to Walk This Out Practically

- **Invite His song.** In prayer, ask the Spirit to place His melody in your heart. Sing what you sense, even if it is simple or wordless.

- **Sing Scripture.** Turn psalms or verses into melodies. This aligns your voice with His Word.

109

- **Make room for spontaneity.** Allow unplanned songs in your worship times. Give space for the Spirit's melody.

- **Use songs in warfare.** When facing heaviness or attack, sing out truth until the atmosphere shifts.

- **Minister through song.** Sing over your children, your spouse, or those in need. Release blessing through melody.

- **Listen first.** Worship is not only an expression but response. Take time to be quiet and hear the song He is already singing.

Prayer Activation

Father Yehovah, thank You for the gift of song. Thank You that You sing over me with joy and that Messiah Himself sings in the midst of His people.

Teach me to see worship as more than melody. Let my singing cut down lies, prune away sin, and open the way for Your Spirit to move.

Yeshua, let me hear Your voice in the congregation and join with You in the eternal song of heaven.

Holy Spirit, fill my worship with Your presence. Let God - singing flow through me as both intimacy with You and a weapon of victory.

Amen.

Bibliography

Baca, Janice F. 2024. *Demons, Devils, Deities: And The Four Witnesses*. Hondo, Texas.

Baca, Janice. 2024. *The Scroll of Mysteries: Cochin Hebrew Revelation*. Second Edition. Hondo, Texas.

British Royal Museum in London, Royal MS 16 A II.

Brooke, George J. "Power to the Powerless - A Long - Lost Song of Miriam," *Biblical Archaeology Review* 20 (1994): 62–65. The Miriam fragment is published in Sidnie A. White, "4Q364 and 365: A Preliminary Report," in The Madrid Qumran Conference, eds. J. Trebolle Barrera and L. Vegas Montaner, Studies in the Text of the Desert of Judah 11 (Leiden: Brill; Madrid: Editorial Complutense, 1992).

Brown, Francis, S R Driver, Charles A Briggs, Edward Robinson, James Strong, and Wilhelm Gesenius. 2015. *The Brown, Driver, Briggs Hebrew and English Lexicon: With an Appendix Containing the Biblical Aramaic: Coded with the Numbering System from Strong's Exhaustive Concordance of the Bible*. Peabody, Mass.: Hendrickson Publishers.

Chaim Bentorah. 2023. "Hebrew Word Study – a Pruning Praise – Zamar - Chaim Bentorah." Chaim Bentorah. April 5, 2023. https://www.chaimbentorah.com/2023/04/hebrew - word - study - a - pruning - praise - zamar/.

"DigiVatLib." 2025. Vatlib.it. 2025. https://digi.vatlib.it/view/MSS_Vat.ebr.100/0007.

Fritz, C.E. 2017. "Psalms, Hymns, or Spiritual Songs?: A Millennial's Journey with the Worship Wars." Honours thesis: Southeastern University

G Johannes Botterweck, and Helmer Ringgren. 1980. *Theological Dictionary of the Old Testament*. Grand Rapids, Mich.: William B. Eerdmans Pub. Co. See link for a free download all 17 vols: https://archive.org/details/theological - dictionary - of - the - old - testament/Theological%20Dictionary%20of%20the%20Old%20Tes tament%20 - %2001/.

Hames, Harvey J. 2012. "Translated from Catalan: Looking at a Fifteenth - Century Hebrew Version of the Gospels," January, 285–302.

Jones, M. 2021. *The Epistle of James (Ya'akov): A Translation from the Hebrew*. Edited by Pam Lutzker and Jonathan Felt. Kerrville, Texas: B'nai Emunah Institute for Accelerated Learning.

Jou̇ on, Paul, and Takamitsu Muraoka. 2005. *A Grammar of Biblical Hebrew*. Roma: Ed. Pontificio Istituto Biblico.

Ludwig Köhler, and Walter Baumgartner. 2001. *The Hebrew and Aramaic Lexicon of the Old Testament*. Hebrew and Aramaic in contact. In: R. Hasselbach - Andee (Ed.), A companion to Ancient Near Eastern languages. Blackwell.

Malloch, S. and Trevarthen, C. 2018. "The Human Nature of Music." Frontiers in Psychology 9:1680.

Municipal Archives of Marseille, Marseille, France Ms. 48.

"Neues Testament in Hebräischer Übersetzung [S. L.], 1563) (Universitätsbibliothek Freiburg I. Br., Hs. 314) - Digital Collections Freiburg - University Library Freiburg." 2025. Uni -

Freiburg.de. 2025. https://dl.ub.uni -
freiburg.de/diglit/hs314?ui_lang=eng.

"Paris. Bibliothèque Sainte - Geneviève, Ms. 131 | Biblissima."
2025. Biblissima.fr. 2025. Website:
https://portail.biblissima.fr/en/ark:/43093/mdata62ef2966f5fc2ec579
d00a3175d46415cad214d0.

Smith, Timothy. 2019. "Review of The Piel Stem System." River
Valley Conference of the Minnesota District, February 2019, 6-8.

Wilhelm Gesenius and Samuel Prideaux Tregelles. 1979.
*Gesenius' Hebrew and Chaldee Lexicon to the Old Testament
Scriptures*. Grand Rapids, Mich.: Baker Book House. Copyright.

Yende, S.J. and Moshugi, K.S. 2024. "Gospel Music As an
Intervention for Peace and Social Change in South Africa."
International Journal of Religion 5(11):5192–5200.

[1] Spiritual gifts are found in the following verses: 1 Corinthians
12:4-11, 28; Ephesians 4:11-16, and Romans 12:6-8.

[2] Daniel 12:4.

[3] Wilhelm Gesenius and Samuel Prideaux Tregelles. 1979.
*Gesenius' Hebrew and Chaldee Lexicon to the Old Testament
Scriptures*. Grand Rapids, Mich.: Baker Book House. Copyright.

[4] Brown, Francis, S R Driver, Charles A Briggs, Edward
Robinson, James Strong, and Wilhelm Gesenius. 2015. *The
Brown, Driver, Briggs Hebrew and English Lexicon: With an
Appendix Containing the Biblical Aramaic: Coded with the*

Numbering System from Strong's Exhaustive Concordance of the Bible. Peabody, Mass.: Hendrickson Publishers.

[5] G Johannes Botterweck, and Helmer Ringgren. 1980. *Theological Dictionary of the Old Testament*. Grand Rapids, Mich.: William B. Eerdmans Pub. Co. See link for a free download all 17 vols: https://archive.org/details/theological - dictionary - of - the - old - testament/Theological%20Dictionary%20of%20the%20Old%20Testament%20 - %2001/

[6] Ludwig Köhler, and Walter Baumgartner. 2001. *The Hebrew and Aramaic Lexicon of the Old Testament*. Hebrew and Aramaic in contact. In: R. Hasselbach - Andee (Ed.), A companion to Ancient Near Eastern languages. Blackwell.

[7] Ludwig Köhler, and Walter Baumgartner. 2001. *The Hebrew and Aramaic Lexicon of the Old Testament*. Hebrew and Aramaic in contact. In: R. Hasselbach - Andee (Ed.), A companion to Ancient Near Eastern languages, (pp. 439-455). Blackwell.

[8] Jou on, Paul, and Takamitsu Muraoka. 2005. *A Grammar of Biblical Hebrew*. Roma: Ed. Pontificio Istituto Biblico, 140.

[9] Smith, Timothy. 2019. "Review of The Piel Stem System." River Valley Conference of the Minnesota District, February 2019, 6-8.

[10] The Archaic form is also found in Exodus 15:2, Psalm 118:14, and Isaiah 12:2.

[11] Chaim Bentorah. 2023. "Hebrew Word Study – a Pruning Praise – Zamar - Chaim Bentorah." Chaim Bentorah. April 5, 2023. https://www.chaimbentorah.com/2023/04/hebrew-word-study-a- pruning-praise-zamar/.

[12] George J. Brooke, "Power to the Powerless - A Long - Lost Song of Miriam," *Biblical Archaeology Review* 20 (1994): 62–65. The Miriam fragment is published in Sidnie A. White, "4Q364 and 365: A Preliminary Report," in The Madrid Qumran Conference, eds. J. Trebolle Barrera and L. Vegas Montaner, Studies in the Text of the Desert of Judah 11 (Leiden: Brill; Madrid: Editorial Complutense, 1992), 217–228 [222–224].

[13] Mizmorim Psalms are as follows: Psalm 1, 3, 4, 5, 6, 8, 9, 12, 13, 15, 19, 20, 21, 22, 23, 24, 29, 30, 31, 38, 39, 40, 41, 47, 48, 49, 50, 51, 62, 63, 64, 65, 66, 67, 68, 75, 75, 76, 77, 79, 82, 83, 84, 85, 87, 88, 92, 98, 100, 101, 108, 110, 139, 140, 141, 143.

[14] Brown, Francis, S R Driver, Charles A Briggs, Edward Robinson, James Strong, and Wilhelm Gesenius. 2015, 664. *The Brown, Driver, Briggs Hebrew and English Lexicon: With an Appendix Containing the Biblical Aramaic: Coded with the Numbering System from Strong's Exhaustive Concordance of the Bible*. Peabody, Mass.: Hendrickson Publishers.

[15] Baca, Janice F. 2024. *Demons, Devils, Deities: And The Four Witnesses*. Hondo, Texas.

[16] Baca, Janice. 2024. *The Scroll of Mysteries: Cochin Hebrew Revelation*. Second Edition. Hondo, Texas.

[17] "Paris. Bibliothèque Sainte - Geneviève, Ms. 131 | Biblissima." 2025. Biblissima.fr. 2025. https://portail.biblissima.fr/en/ark:/43093/mdata62ef2966f5fc2ec579d00a3175d46415cad214d0.

[18] "DigiVatLib." 2025. Vatlib.it. 2025. https://digi.vatlib.it/view/MSS_Vat.ebr.100/0007.

[19] Hames, Harvey J. 2012. "Translated from Catalan: Looking at a Fifteenth - Century Hebrew Version of the Gospels," January, 285–302.

[20] "Neues Testament in Hebräischer Übersetzung ([S. L.], 1563) (Universitätsbibliothek Freiburg I. Br., Hs. 314) - Digital Collections Freiburg - University Library Freiburg." 2025. Uni - Freiburg.de. 2025. https://dl.ub.uni-freiburg.de/diglit/hs314?ui_lang=eng.

[21] "Neues Testament in Hebräischer Übersetzung ([S. L.], 1563) (Universitätsbibliothek Freiburg I. Br., Hs. 314) - Digital Collections Freiburg - University Library Freiburg." 2025. Uni - Freiburg.de. 2025. https://dl.ub.uni-freiburg.de/diglit/hs314?ui_lang=eng.

[22] Municipal Archives of Marseille, Marseille, France Ms. 48.

[23] British Royal Museum in London, Royal MS 16 A II.

[24] Jones, M. 2021. *The Epistle of James (Ya'akov): A Translation from the Hebrew*. Edited by Pam Lutzker and Jonathan Felt. Kerrville, Texas: B'nai Emunah Institute for Accelerated Learning, 10.

Chapter 10: Consecration and Anointing

Before a priest could serve in the holy things, he had to be set apart. Consecration was not optional. It was the visible and tangible act of being marked as holy unto Yehovah. The word *consecrate* means to dedicate, to fill the hands, to transfer from the common to the sacred. Without consecration, no priest could carry out the service of the Tabernacle or Temple.

This pattern reveals an important truth: before we can serve Messiah faithfully, our lives must be consecrated. We cannot minister in the holy things while clinging to what is unholy. We cannot walk in the Spirit while being driven by the flesh. Consecration is the foundation of priesthood. It is how we move from ordinary living into a life marked by His presence.

Anointing with Oil Before Service

Exodus 29:7 describes the moment Aaron was anointed: "Then you shall take the anointing oil, and pour it on his head and anoint him." This was no gentle dab of oil. The psalmist tells us that the oil ran down Aaron's beard and onto his garments (Psalm 133:2). This abundance showed the lavish work of the Spirit. The oil was costly, fragrant, and sacred. Exodus 30 explains that its formula could not be duplicated for personal use. To be anointed was to be sealed with Yah's presence and authority.

Each ingredient in the anointing oil carried meaning:

- **Myrrh** represented death to self and the sweetness of surrender.

- **Cinnamon** symbolized passion and zeal for God.

117

- **Calamus** pointed to uprightness and integrity.

- **Cassia** spoke of humility and submission.

- **Olive oil** was the base, representing the Spirit who carries all of these qualities.

Together, they teach us that consecration requires death to self, zeal for Yah, uprightness, humility, and dependence on the Spirit. The fragrance of the anointing was so distinct that anyone who smelled it knew a priest had been in the presence of God.

For us, the Spirit's anointing is what sets us apart. We are not anointed for comfort but for calling. David was empowered by the Spirit to lead. The disciples were empowered to witness boldly at Pentecost. We, too, are empowered to live consecrated lives that reveal Messiah to the world.

Laying on of Hands for Holy Tasks

Consecration also involved the laying on of hands. This was more than a ritual. It was identification and transfer. In sacrifices, hands placed on the animal represented the transfer of sin. In consecration, hands placed on the priest represented the transfer of blessing, authority, and calling.

Moses laid his hands on Joshua, passing on leadership with visible confirmation (Numbers 27:18 - 23). The apostles laid hands on believers for healing, on deacons for service, and on missionaries for sending (Acts 6:6; Acts 13:3). Paul reminded Timothy that his gift was imparted "through the laying on of hands" (1 Timothy 4:14).

This shows us that consecration is not just personal; it is communal. It is affirmed by the body. No one consecrates themselves for ministry in isolation. Yehovah uses His people to confirm His calling. To lay hands is to say, "We recognize what God has placed in you, and we stand with you in it."

When we resist accountability or reject the body's confirmation, we miss part of what consecration provides. True consecration is both vertical (set apart unto God) and horizontal (affirmed by His people).

Consecration as a Life Pattern

Consecration was not a one-time event. The priests were consecrated at their ordination, but they were also called to live consecrated daily. Garments had to be kept holy. Washings had to be performed. Sacrifices had to be offered continually. Consecration was ongoing.

This teaches us that consecration is both moment and lifestyle. Yes, there are defining moments when God sets us apart. But there must also be daily choices to remain set apart. Consecration affects what we wear spiritually (our garments of righteousness), how we cleanse ourselves (through confession and repentance), and how we present ourselves (as living sacrifices, Romans 12:1).

It is easy to slip back into the common. Israel often did. But priests were called to stand out, not blend in. The same is true for us. Our consecration should be evident in our choices, speech, values, and worship. We are called to be holy because He is holy (1 Peter 1:16).

Messiah - Life Parallel: Living Anointed and Set Apart

Yeshua is the ultimate picture of consecration. At His baptism, the Spirit descended and remained on Him, anointing Him for ministry. In Luke 4, He declared, "The Spirit of the Lord is upon Me, because He has anointed Me to proclaim good news to the poor." He lived every moment consecrated to the Father's will, empowered by the Spirit to heal, deliver, and save.

In Him, we share that consecration. Peter calls us "a chosen generation, a royal priesthood, a holy nation" (1 Peter 2:9). We have been anointed by the Spirit (1 John 2:20, 27). Our consecration means our lives are no longer our own. We have been bought with a price and set apart for His glory.

This is not limited to ministry platforms. Consecration shows up in daily life - in parenting, in how we work, in how we treat our neighbors, in how we guard holiness in our homes. Wherever we go, the fragrance of the anointing should be evident. Consecration is not about titles; it is about living as priests of Yah every day.

Teaching Takeaways

- Consecration means to be set apart, both in a moment and as a lifestyle.

- The anointing oil pointed to the Spirit and the qualities of a consecrated life: surrender, zeal, uprightness, humility, and dependence on Him.

- Laying on of hands showed that consecration is both personal and communal. It affirms calling and imparts blessing.

- Consecration must be maintained daily, not treated as a one - time event.

- Yeshua is the Anointed One, and in Him we share His consecration by the Spirit.

Reflections for the Reader

- Are there areas of your life still mixed with the common that need to be set apart for Yehovah?

- Do people sense the fragrance of consecration in your words, actions, and presence?

- Who has affirmed your calling through the laying on of hands, and how have you honored that commissioning?

- Are you living consecrated daily, or do you treat consecration as a moment in the past rather than a lifestyle now?

- How would your life change if you saw yourself as anointed and consecrated for every sphere you walk into, not just "ministry"?

How to Walk This Out Practically

- **Renew consecration daily.** Begin each day with a prayer of surrender, dedicating yourself afresh to Yah's service.

- **Guard what is holy.** Refuse to use your anointing for selfish or worldly purposes. Keep your gifts set apart for His glory.

- **Seek the Spirit's filling.** Ask regularly for fresh oil - the Spirit's presence and empowerment in your life.

- **Honor community.** Welcome the laying on of hands and affirmation from trusted leaders who can recognize and bless your calling.

- **Live distinctly.** Make intentional choices that show you belong to Yah - in speech, conduct, and integrity.

- **Stay available.** Consecration is not about position but posture. Keep saying "yes" when the Father calls you into service.

Prayer Activation

Father Yehovah, thank You for calling me into Your service. I offer myself to You in consecration. Set me apart from what is common and make me holy unto You.

Pour out Your Spirit on me as the oil was poured on Aaron. Let the fragrance of Your anointing fill my life with surrender, zeal, uprightness, humility, and dependence on You.

Yeshua, You are the Anointed One. Teach me to live in Your consecration, empowered by the Spirit to proclaim good news, bring healing, and release freedom wherever You send me.

Holy Spirit, confirm my calling and strengthen me daily. Help me live not as one who was consecrated once, but as one who is continually set apart for Your purposes. May my life carry the fragrance of consecration and the authority of the anointing everywhere I go.

Amen.

Chapter 11: Blessing the People

When the priests completed their service, after cleansing themselves, tending the altar, and offering the sacrifices, they did not end in silence. Their final act was to lift their hands and bless the people. The words they spoke were not human comfort or polite farewell; they were divine decree.

"Yehovah bless you and keep you;
Yehovah make His face shine upon you and be gracious to you;
Yehovah lift up His countenance upon you and give you peace."
(Numbers 6:24-26)

This was not a suggestion, but a command from Yehovah Himself. Through the blessing, His Name was placed upon Israel, and His presence was promised among them. The priests had prepared the altar, purified themselves, and guarded the fire, but this was the culmination of it all. Priestly ministry always ends in blessing. Every act of sacrifice, cleansing, and intercession pointed toward this sacred moment when the people would be covered with Yah's favor, peace, and protection.

The Power of the Priestly Voice

In Hebrew thought, *barak* (to bless) carries the sense of God stooping down in grace and favor. When the priest spoke the blessing, he was not merely reciting words; he was releasing heaven's authority into the earth. The hands lifted in blessing mirrored the hands once used in sacrifice. Both were extensions of service, one offering atonement and the other releasing life.

The priest's role did not end at the altar. Having been purified by fire and water, he became a vessel through which Yehovah's

124

presence could flow to the people. Blessing was the natural outflow of holiness. A clean heart speaks clean words.

Each time a priest spoke the blessing, the atmosphere changed. The people left marked by God's Name, identified as His own, and enveloped by His shalom.

Pronouncing the Aaronic Blessing

Numbers 6:24-26 records the words Yah commanded Aaron and his sons to speak:

1. **Yevarechecha Yehovah v'yishmerecha** - "Yehovah bless you and keep you."

   o *Yevarechecha* (יְבָרֶכְךָ): from *barak*, to bless or to kneel. It pictures God stooping to pour favor into your life.

   o *V'yishmerecha* (וְיִשְׁמְרֶךָ): from *shamar*, to guard, protect, or keep watch, the same word used when Adam was told to "keep" the garden.
   Application: Blessing declares both Yah's provision and His protection. God gives, and God guards.

2. **Ya'er Yehovah panav eilecha vichuneka** - "Yehovah make His face shine upon you and be gracious to you."

   o *Ya'er* (יָאֵר): from *or*, meaning light. His shining face brings clarity, revelation, and favor.

- o *Panav* (פָּנָיו): face, but also presence and attention.

- o *Vichuneka* (וִיחֻנֶּךָ): from *chanan*, grace freely given.
  Application: To bless in this way is to call for God's presence to draw near, flooding a life with grace and understanding.

3. **Yisa Yehovah panav eilecha v'yasem lecha shalom** - "Yehovah lift up His countenance upon you and give you peace."

- o *Yisa* (יִשָּׂא): to lift up or show delight, like a father smiling at his child.

- o *Shalom* (שָׁלוֹם): wholeness, completeness, health, prosperity, and harmony under Yah's order.
  Application: This is the climax of the blessing, God's delight resting on His people, bringing wholeness and divine order.

The structure of the blessing itself grows in intensity, three Hebrew words, then five, then seven. The grace multiplies with each line, showing that Yah's blessing does not diminish; it expands.

Speaking Yehovah's Name Over the People

Numbers 6:27 declares, "So shall they put My Name upon the people of Israel, and I will bless them." This was not a benediction; it was a spiritual sealing. To speak Yah's Name over the people marked them as His possession and invited His presence to dwell among them.

For the priest, this was the highest privilege. He was not only to bear God's Name; he was to bestow it. His voice became the conduit of divine identity, declaring who the people were and whose they were.

To bear His Name meant identity, protection, and presence:

- **Identity:** They belonged to Yehovah.

- **Protection:** His Name covered them like a royal seal.

- **Presence:** His Name signified His nearness.

Messiah's Life Parallel: Yeshua the Blessing High Priest

Yeshua embodied the priestly blessing in every part of His ministry. He was the face of God shining upon Israel, the living revelation of divine grace and truth. His words healed, His touch restored, and His presence brought peace.

After His resurrection, He lifted His hands and blessed His disciples. "And it came to pass, while He blessed them, He was parted from them and carried up into heaven" (Luke 24:50-51). His final act before ascending was to bless. The same hands that bore the marks of sacrifice now released the power of life.

As priests in Messiah, we carry this same calling. When we bless, we place His Name upon people and release His covenant promises. Our words seal identity, impart peace, and war against the lies of the enemy. Blessing is not sentimental; it is spiritual warfare, declaring ownership of souls that belong to Yah.

Teaching Takeaways

- The Aaronic Blessing is a command from Yah, not a tradition of men.

- Each phrase reveals Yah's increasing favor, protection, presence, and peace.

- To speak His Name is to seal identity and invite His dwelling.

- Yeshua fulfilled this blessing and passed it to His followers to continue.

- Blessing is priestly warfare; it covers, marks, and defends those under His Name.

Reflections for the Reader

- Do you see blessing as optional, or as your priestly duty?

- How often do you intentionally speak Yehovah's Name over your family or congregation?

- Have your words reflected blessing or curse, identity or confusion?

- Who around you needs to hear the reminder, "You belong to Yah"?

How to Walk This Out Practically

- **Bless your household.** Speak Numbers 6:24-26 daily over your family. Make it part of your rhythm of worship.

- **Bless your community.** When gathering with others, pronounce the blessing before leaving. Cover them with Yah's Name.

- **Guard your tongue.** Refuse gossip or negativity. If you speak carelessly, replace it with a declaration of blessing.

- **Mark in prayer.** As you intercede, declare Yah's Name over homes, workplaces, and leaders.

- **Bless beyond comfort.** Speak peace even to enemies. You are not condoning behavior; you are reclaiming identity.

- **Model it for the next generation.** Teach your children how to bless their siblings and friends. This shapes a priestly culture in your home.

Prayer Activation

Father Yehovah, thank You for the privilege of carrying and speaking Your Name. As I bless others, let Your presence rest upon them. Make my words vessels of Your light and peace. Teach me to guard my tongue so that everything I speak brings life, healing, and identity. Let my home, my church, and my community be covered with Your Name and filled with Your shalom.

Yeshua, You are the blessing made flesh. When I lift my hands to bless, let Your Spirit move through me as it did through You.

Holy Spirit, empower me to speak not from emotion but from truth. Let every blessing I declare become a seal of covenant and a barrier against the enemy's schemes.

May Your face shine upon me, and through me, that others may see Your goodness and give You glory.

In the Name of Yeshua, Amen.

Chapter 12: Restoring the Outcast - Cleansing the Leper and Restoring the Defiled

The priests of Israel were not only guardians of holiness; they were agents of restoration. Leviticus 14 gives detailed instructions for the cleansing of a leper, a process that combined sacrifice, ceremony, and compassion. It was one of the few priestly duties that brought reconciliation between the outcast and the community.

Cleansing the Leper

When a person was healed of leprosy, he could not simply return to life as usual. He was required to present himself to the priest, who alone had authority to declare him clean. The priest examined him, verified the healing, and then began a seven-day process that symbolized complete restoration. Two birds were brought as an offering: one slain over running water, the other dipped in the blood and released into the open field.

This vivid act spoke of both death and life, one life given and another set free. The priest then sprinkled the blood seven times upon the one being cleansed, shaved his hair, washed his garments, and declared him clean. On the eighth day, the man brought sacrifices to the door of the Tabernacle, and the priest anointed him with blood and oil upon the right ear, the thumb of the right hand, and the big toe of the right foot. These were the same anointing points used for consecrating priests themselves (Leviticus 8:23-24).

The message was unmistakable. The restored outcast was being re-consecrated for service and re-anointed for life within the covenant community.

The Heart of Restoration

This ritual revealed the Father's heart. While sin and uncleanness separated people from His presence, His desire was always to restore. The priest's role was not to condemn but to confirm cleansing. He acted as Yah's representative, extending grace through obedience to His command.

In every generation, the leper represents those who have been pushed outside the camp: the wounded, the rejected, the shamed, and those marked unclean by sin or circumstance. True priesthood still bears the responsibility of seeking them out and declaring the possibility of renewal.

Holiness and mercy are not opposites; they are partners. The same priest who guarded purity also carried the power to restore. Holiness without compassion hardens into pride, and compassion without holiness loses truth. The priest was called to carry both.

Messiah's Fulfillment

When Yeshua healed the leper in Luke 5:12-14, He told him, "Go and show yourself to the priest, and make an offering for your cleansing, as Moses commanded, for a testimony to them." Yeshua honored the Torah's order even while embodying its ultimate fulfillment. He was not abolishing the priestly process. He was showing that true cleansing flows from the Word made flesh.

Every act of healing Yeshua performed was an act of restoration. He touched the untouchable, spoke to the rejected, and brought near those who had been cast away. His command to show the priest confirmed that He had not come to discard the system but to complete it. The priest could declare clean what Yeshua had already made whole.

In Yeshua, every leper finds both healer and high priest. He not only restores the body but reinstates the person, giving them back dignity, belonging, and purpose.

Modern Priestly Ministry

For believers today, this becomes a picture of pastoral care and reconciliation ministry. We are called to restore those who have fallen, not to exclude them indefinitely. Paul wrote, "If anyone is caught in a trespass, you who are spiritual should restore such a one in a spirit of gentleness" (Galatians 6:1). Restoration is priestly work.

Our world is full of spiritual lepers, those scarred by sin, guilt, or rejection. Some carry visible wounds, others hide invisible ones. The priest's role has not changed. We are to move toward the hurting, speak life where shame has silenced, and declare cleansing through the blood of Messiah.

To restore the defiled is to partner with Heaven's redemptive heart. The same Spirit that sanctifies also reconciles. The priest who once pronounced "unclean" must now be the first to speak "clean" when the power of God has brought renewal.

Teaching Takeaways

- The priest's authority to declare clean was a sacred trust that restored people to covenant life.

- The cleansing ritual pointed to Yeshua, who heals, forgives, and reinstates the outcast.

- Holiness and mercy must work together in every act of ministry.

- Spiritual leprosy today appears as bitterness, shame, addiction, or sin, but the blood of Messiah still cleanses.

- True priesthood does not avoid the broken; it moves toward them.

Messiah's Life Parallel: The Healer Who Restores

Yeshua reached beyond the boundaries of purity laws not to break them but to reveal their heart. He touched the leper, not to become defiled, but to make the defiled pure. He restored sight, cleansed hearts, and brought near those the world had abandoned. Every time He said, "Be clean," He echoed the priestly declaration of Leviticus 14, but with eternal authority.

The same Spirit that moved through Him now moves through us. When we forgive, comfort, and restore, we echo the voice of our High Priest.

Reflections for the Reader

- Who in your life has been treated like an outcast?

- Do you tend to avoid the defiled or move toward them in mercy?

- Have you allowed the blood of Messiah to cleanse your own shame and restore your confidence before Him?

- What would it look like to act as a priest of reconciliation in your home, church, or workplace?

How to Walk This Out Practically

- **Reach out to the hurting.** Make space for those who feel rejected or forgotten. Listen, pray, and speak hope.

- **Declare cleansing, not condemnation.** When you see repentance and renewal, affirm what God has done.

- **Practice gentle restoration.** Approach those who have fallen with truth and compassion, not judgment.

- **Carry the oil and blood.** The oil represents the Spirit's empowerment; the blood, Messiah's atonement. Both are needed to bring people back to wholeness.

- **Stay humble.** Remember that every priest was once in need of cleansing too. Restoration flows best through those who know grace firsthand.

Prayer Activation

Father Yehovah, thank You that You are the God who restores.
You do not cast away the broken; You call them back to life. Teach
me to walk as a priest of reconciliation, to speak cleansing where
there has been shame, and to declare wholeness where there has
been rejection.

Yeshua, thank You for touching the unclean and making them
whole. Let Your compassion move through me to those the world
avoids.

Holy Spirit, give me discernment to see who needs restoration and
courage to act in love. Let every word I speak bring healing,
renewal, and peace.

Make me a vessel of Your mercy so that the outcast may find their
place again among Your people.

In the Name of Yeshua, Amen.

Chapter 13: Putting It All Together - A Priestly Life

We've journeyed together through the priestly service, from the daily offerings to the blessing of the people. Each chapter has revealed another glimpse of what it meant for Israel's priests to serve Yehovah and what it means for us as priests in Messiah.

Now we come to the moment where every piece comes together. The garments, the sacrifices, the oil, the incense, the bread, the feasts, and the ministry of restoration all point to one greater reality: the priesthood was never meant to be ritual alone. It was preparation for relationship. Every act, every offering, every cleansing was training in how to carry the presence of Yehovah with reverence, purity, and purpose.

In ancient Israel, a young Levite began training for priestly service five years before he was allowed to minister at the altar. Five, the number of grace, marked his season of preparation. Before he ever touched the holy things, he learned how to live a holy life. Grace trained him to serve. Grace prepared him to stand.

And now that same call reaches you. This journey through *The Priestly Service* has not been mere study; it has been your invitation into that same training. You have been called into a Royal Priesthood, a life set apart to carry His presence into the world. Your preparation begins now. Let His Spirit begin to establish these truths in your daily walk, morning by morning, choice by choice, step by step.

This is more than history. It is your commission. The same God who called Aaron to stand between the living and the dead now calls you to rise and serve as His priest in this generation. The

137

training begins today, and the grace to fulfill it has already been given.

A Life on the Altar

Priesthood begins with surrender. Every morning and evening, the altar burned with fire. For us, that means our lives are bookended by devotion. Start the day by laying yourself on the altar, and end the day by entrusting it all back to Him. Constancy, not convenience, is the rhythm of priesthood.

A Life of Holiness

Priests stayed clean, their garments, their bodies, their service. For us, it's the call to guard the garments of righteousness Messiah has given. Holiness is not optional. It is the posture of those who serve in His presence.

A Life of Restoration

Leviticus 14 shows that priests were not only guardians of holiness but agents of healing. They examined the leper, declared cleansing, and restored the defiled to covenant fellowship. Yeshua modeled this perfectly when He touched the unclean, made them whole, and gave dignity back to the broken. In Him, the priestly call became personal. Restoration is not a side ministry but the heart of priesthood. Holiness prepares you to be clean; restoration teaches you to make others whole.

A Life of Light and Bread

The menorah lit the way; the bread fed the priests. Together they point us to the Spirit and the Word. Without the Spirit, we cannot see. Without the Word, we cannot stand. Your priestly life depends on trimming the wicks, replenishing the oil, and presenting the Bread to others.

A Life of Teaching and Judging

Priests taught the people and judged disputes with Yah's Word. You too are called to disciple others, to guide with clarity, and to walk in discernment. Do not shrink from teaching the basics of the faith. Do not be silent when discernment is needed. Your priestly voice is meant to bring truth in love.

A Life in Yah's Rhythm

Priests led Israel through the feasts and carried the Ark of His presence. You are called to live by Yah's calendar, to remember His appointed times, and to prepare others for the prophetic fulfillment to come. And as you walk, you carry His presence into the world as His ambassador.

A Life of Guarding

Adam failed to guard the garden, but priests were commanded to guard the gates. Guard your heart. Guard your home. Guard the purity of the faith. What Yah entrusts to you is holy. Carry it with reverence.

A Life of Worship

Music was not entertainment; it was ministry. Priests sang psalms, played instruments, and shifted atmospheres. You are called to the same. Worship is warfare. Worship is healing. Worship is ministry before His presence. Let your life itself become a psalm rising to heaven.

A Life of Blessing

Priestly service ended with blessing. Hands lifted, the Name of Yehovah spoken, the people marked as His. Your calling is the same. End your conversations, your gatherings, and your family rhythms with blessing. Speak His Name. Place His seal on those entrusted to you.

Pulling It All Together

This is the priestly life in Messiah:

A life on the altar.
A life of holiness.
A life of restoration.
A life of light and bread.
A life of teaching and discernment.
A life lived in His rhythm, carrying His presence.
A life of guarding what is holy.
A life of worship that shifts atmospheres.
A life of blessing that marks people with His Name.

This is not theory. It is your calling. Messiah has made you part of His royal priesthood. And the world desperately needs priests who live this way.

Teaching Takeaways

- Priesthood is not an ancient ritual but a present calling.

- Each duty points to Messiah and calls us into practical service today.

- Restoration is central to priestly ministry; holiness and compassion must walk together.

- To live as priests is to embody surrender, holiness, restoration, light, bread, teaching, guarding, worship, and blessing.

- This life is not optional. It is the design of God for His people in Messiah.

Reflections for the Reader

- Which area of priestly life is strongest in me right now? Which area needs renewal?

- Have I embraced restoration as part of my calling, or have I avoided the broken?

- Do I see myself as part of a royal priesthood, or am I still living as a bystander?

- How might my family, congregation, and community change if I lived fully as a priest in Messiah?

- Who is waiting for me to step into this calling, to intercede, to restore, to bless, to carry His presence?

How to Walk This Out Practically

- **Rise daily.** Start and end your day with surrender at the altar.

- **Stay clean.** Keep your garments pure through repentance and the washing of the Word.

- **Reach and restore.** Move toward those who feel unworthy or forgotten. Speak cleansing, not condemnation.

- **Fuel the flame.** Replenish the oil of the Spirit and trim away what dims your light.

- **Feed and teach.** Nourish yourself in the Word and share it faithfully with others.

- **Live by His rhythm.** Mark the feasts and let them shape your calendar and your hope.

- **Guard well.** Protect your home, your heart, and your community from compromise.

- **Worship boldly.** Use song, prayer, and praise as tools of warfare and healing.

- **Bless often.** Speak Yah's Name over your family, your friends, and your community. Seal them in His covenant identity.

-

Prayer Activation

Father Yehovah, thank You for calling me into Your royal priesthood. I receive this calling not as history but as my life. Yeshua, You are my High Priest and my example. Teach me to live surrendered, holy, and full of Your light. Make me a restorer of the broken and a healer of the outcast.

Holy Spirit, empower me to guard, to teach, to worship, to bless, and to restore. Mark my life as a living sacrifice, a keeper of the flame, a carrier of Your presence, and a voice of blessing in the world.

Here I am, Lord. Consecrated. Anointed. Sent.

I rise into my priestly calling today.

Amen.

You've prayed it, you've declared it, now it's time to live it. What you've read in this book isn't meant to stay on the page. It's meant to shape your steps, guide your choices, and mark your life as one who walks in the Spirit. Take these truths and begin practicing them in the ordinary moments of your day. That's where priestly service really shines, not only in the "big" moments but in the quiet faithfulness of living set apart for Him.

And don't keep this to yourself. Just as you've craved understanding and longed for clarity on how to walk this out, others are hungry too. Share what you're learning, in conversations, in prayer groups, with family and friends. The message of Yeshua as our High Priest, and of our calling as a royal priesthood, is not one to be hoarded. It's one to be multiplied.

Remember: the priestly calling was never designed to be carried alone. Israel's priests served together, shoulder to shoulder, in the presence of Yehovah. In the same way, you are part of a larger body, the living stones being built together into His dwelling place. As you step forward, do it with boldness, knowing that your walk may be the encouragement someone else has been waiting for.

So go and live as the priest you were called to be, letting your life become a sanctuary where His presence is known. With every step you take in priestly service, remember that you are testifying that Yeshua lives in you. Walk it out with joy, and let His light in you awaken a hunger for Him in others.

Selah, Shema, & Shalom
Jeff
The Way Remnant

About The Author

Jeff Brannon hails from the Piney Woods of Northeast Texas, along the shores of Caddo Lake. He surrendered his life to Christ at fifteen and has faithfully served in ministry for over 36 years. His journey has taken him from Youth Pastor and Evangelist to a four-year tenure as Senior Pastor of Caddo Lake Church in Uncertain, Texas … the very congregation where he first encountered Jesus as Lord.

Driven by a passion for biblical teaching and apologetics, Jeff delights in helping others understand and defend their faith. Together with his wife, Miranda, he leads The Way Remnant - an online ministry reaching audiences on YouTube, Facebook, TikTok, X, and Rumble. They also provide marriage counseling and host regular gatherings in their West Virginia home.

Connect with Jeff and Miranda at TheWayRemnant@gmail.com.

Visit our website:

TheWayRemnant.com

See us on YouTube:
http://YouTube.com/TheWayRemnant

Check out these other books by Jeff:

#JeffWroteABook

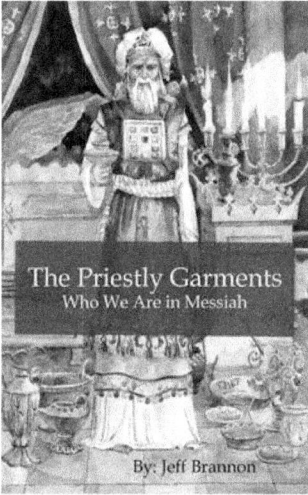

The Priestly Garments: Who We Are in Messiah
A Thirty - Year Exploration of Levitical Divine Vestments
 Dive into a lifetime of discovery as you explore the sacred attire prescribed in Leviticus - garments that reveal not only the ancient world of Israel's tabernacle but also the heart of Messiah's work on our behalf. What began as a spark of curiosity at a Wednesday night youth service has grown into a comprehensive study of Hebrew language, Near Eastern culture, and biblical typology, offering fresh insights on every fold of the priestly robes.

Why This Book Matters
 Each chapter walks you through the original Hebrew terms and cultural contexts, illuminating how every color, thread count, and gemstone speaks of promises purchased at Calvary. You'll see how a pastor's teenage fascination became a scholarly pilgrimage, culminating in layered commentary that bridges ancient ritual and modern devotion.

Equip Yourself for Deeper Study
 Whether you're a student of Scripture, a teacher in the church, or

someone longing for intimacy with the Creator, these pages will become a roadmap for encountering God's design "from the very beginning." Let the priestly garments clothe your understanding - opening doors to richer worship, profound healing, and unshakeable identity in Messiah.

Claim the truths woven into every stitch and stand fortified by the promises our Creator ordained before time began.

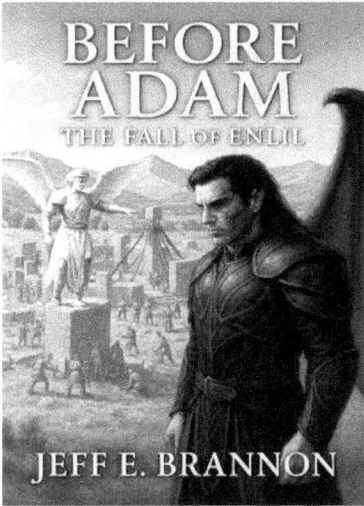

Book 1 of The Watcher's Trilogy

Before Adam: The Fall of Enlil is a gripping theological novel that dares to explore the ancient war before time - a cosmic rebellion that set the stage for everything we know about good and evil, Eden and exile, heaven and earth.

Long before the creation of Adam, before the first sunrise, there was light - pure, holy, divine. And in that Light walked Enlil, a majestic angel created with brilliance, music, and purpose. But pride swelled within him. What began as a question became a challenge. What became a challenge became war.

This is the story of a rebellion in the heavens - a celestial uprising led not by a monster, but by one who once worshiped at the throne of Yehovah. Before Adam weaves together ancient biblical imagery, forgotten texts, and rich speculative theology to tell the story of how beauty became corruption, and how the seeds of deception were planted long before Eve ever met the serpent.

149

As the angels choose sides and the fabric of creation trembles, Enlil faces judgment - but not as expected. His punishment is not immediate destruction, but a deeper sentence: to witness, from the dust, the unfolding plan of redemption, mercy, and glory that he once rejected.

This book is not just fiction - it's a bold reimagining that invites readers to consider the spiritual warfare behind the veil, the justice and mercy of a holy God, and the prophetic truths embedded in the Genesis narrative.

Before Adam is perfect for readers who love theological depth, epic storytelling, and thought-provoking insights into Scripture. Whether you're a scholar, a seeker, or simply captivated by the mysteries of creation, this story will challenge what you thought you knew - and draw you into a war that still echoes today.

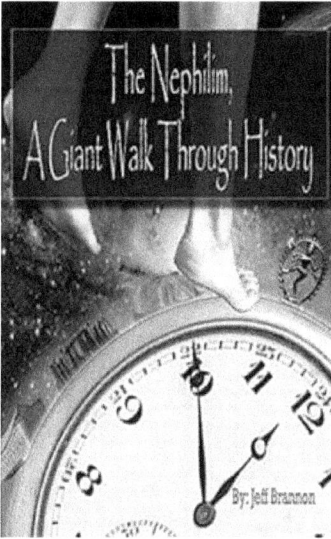

The Nephilim, A Giant Walk Through History
Book 2 of The Watcher's Trilogy

A sweeping, biblically grounded adventure that begins with Jared, Noah's grandfather, and races through history into the modern day - revealing the hidden legacy of the Nephilim, "those who fell." Born of fallen angels and human women, these giants reshape everything we thought we knew about Scripture and Earth's ancient past. Drawing on canonical texts alongside extra - biblical treasures such as 1 Enoch, Jubilees, Jasher, and the Book of Giants, this story weaves fact and fiction into a thrilling narrative that challenges the reader to ask: If God is love, why did He permit genocide in the Old Testament? What did Jesus mean when He said the end times would mirror Noah's day?

From the rise of Nimrod and his enigmatic queen to the mysterious Vimana described in over a thousand ancient writings, every twist of this tale springs from synchronized, historically endorsed sources including Dead Sea Scroll fragments. You'll witness monumental battles, secret technologies, and angelic councils, all set against a backdrop of real places and events that illuminate questions the modern church often fears to face.

Journey through epochs of wonder and warning, and glimpse of what the near future may hold. Are the Nephilim truly gone, or do they walk among us still? Discover the answers in this extraordinary fusion of scholarship and storytelling - where the past comes alive, the present is transformed, and the future pulses with possibility.

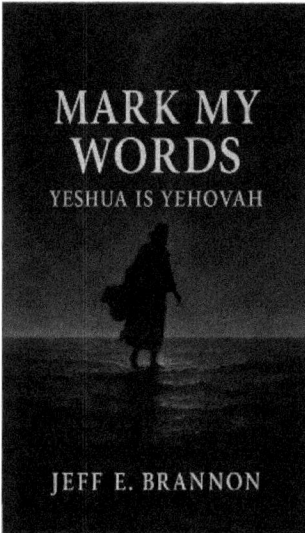

Mark My Words: Yeshua is Yehovah
Unveiling the Divine Identity in the Gospel of Mark

For generations, readers have seen the miracles and teachings of Yeshua without realizing what Mark was truly declaring: the Holy One of Israel Himself walked among His people. In *Mark My Words: Yeshua is Yehovah*, Jeff E. Brannon takes you through the Gospel of Mark verse by verse to uncover the original revelation - Yeshua is not merely sent by Yehovah; He *is* Yehovah revealed in the flesh.

Written from a Hebraic and Spirit-filled perspective, this book restores the ancient understanding that the early believers held with certainty. Brannon shows how Mark's "simple" Gospel carries profound theological precision. Each miracle, confrontation, and act of compassion mirrors Yehovah's own works recorded in the Torah and Prophets. When Yeshua commands the wind and sea, forgives sin, walks on water, and heals the leper, He displays the same authority described of Yehovah throughout Scripture.

Drawing from Hebrew language insights, early manuscript evidence, and the prophetic continuity of the Tanakh, *Mark My Words* bridges scholarship and revelation. It demonstrates how the divine name, nature, and mission of Yehovah are embodied perfectly in Yeshua the Messiah.

This study is not just informational - it's transformational. As you trace each chapter, you'll see the unity of the Father and the Son in action. You'll rediscover the covenant faithfulness of Yehovah expressed through Yeshua's mercy, holiness, and power.

Through this journey you will learn:

- How Mark's structure and language reveal Yeshua as Yehovah in human form.

- Why early followers of Messiah had no struggle affirming His divinity.

- How the Gospel narratives fulfill Yehovah's ancient promises of redemption.

Mark My Words: Yeshua is Yehovah calls you to read the Gospel with new eyes and a restored heart. When you finish, you'll not only know more about Yeshua - you'll recognize Him as the covenant - keeping God who spoke from Sinai, calmed the storm, and still calls His people by name.

Return to Mark's Gospel. Hear His voice. See His glory. Discover that Yeshua is Yehovah.

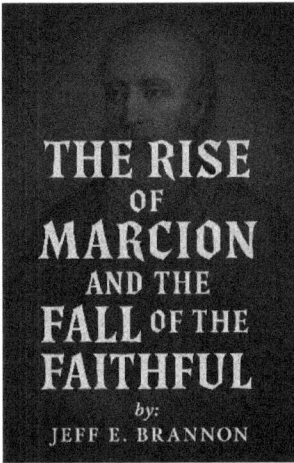

THE RISE
OF
MARCION
AND THE
FALL OF THE
FAITHFUL
by:
JEFF E. BRANNON

Marcion of Sinope is often treated as a minor figure in church history, yet his theology reshaped the faith in lasting ways. He rejected the God of the Hebrew Scriptures, dismissed the Torah, and recast Yeshua as a redeemer disconnected from Israel's covenant story. Though formally condemned, Marcion's ideas did not begin with him, nor did they end with his exile.

This book traces the lineage of Marcion's thinking back to earlier figures such as Simon Magus, Nicolas, Cerinthus, and Valentinus. These men introduced dualism, secret knowledge, antinomianism, and a divided view of God that slowly eroded the apostolic foundation. Marcion did not invent these errors. He systematized them, giving structure to ideas already spreading beneath the surface of the early assemblies.

By examining historical records, early church writings, and Scripture itself, this work exposes how these teachings fractured the believing community and created a false opposition between Torah and grace. What the apostles preached as a unified message of covenant and obedience was replaced with a distorted gospel detached from its Hebraic roots.

155

The book then follows how Marcion's framework quietly reemerged across centuries, shaping modern doctrines that reject the Old Testament, dismiss obedience, and separate Yeshua from the Father's revealed ways. What was once labeled heresy is now often assumed to be orthodox.

The Rise of Marcion and the Fall of the Faithful calls readers to test their beliefs against Scripture and history, and to return to the faith once delivered … a faith rooted in covenant, continuity, and the unchanging character of Yehovah.

A Word from the Publisher

When you finish a book that speaks to your heart, your response matters more than you might think. Reviews are not just feedback; they are a way to share truth, encourage the author, and help others discover what you have found.

Online stores like Amazon use reviews and ratings to decide which books to recommend. The more readers engage, the more visibility a message receives. It is not about popularity; it is about reach. Every time you leave a review, you help the Word go farther than algorithms alone ever could.

If this book encouraged you, taught you something new, or helped you draw closer to Yehovah, please consider taking a moment to share that. Your honest review, even a few simple sentences, can lead someone else to find the same truth that touched your life.

Thank you for being part of this mission to awaken hearts, strengthen faith, and point people back to the fullness of who Yeshua is. Your voice carries farther than you realize.

How to Leave a Review on Amazon

1. Go to Amazon.com and sign in.

2. Search for the book title (for example: *The Priestly Service: How We Walk in the Spirit*).

3. Click on the book cover or title to open the product page.

4. Scroll down until you see Customer Reviews.

5. Click Write a Customer Review.

6. Choose a star rating, then share a few sentences about what you learned or enjoyed.

7. Click Submit and that's it.

It only takes a minute, but it makes a lasting impact.

Thank you for reading, for sharing, and for helping this message reach others who are searching for truth.

www.ingramcontent.com/pod-product-compliance
Lightning Source LLC
LaVergne TN
LVHW052027080426
835513LV00018B/2196